Profits from Your Backyard Herb Garden

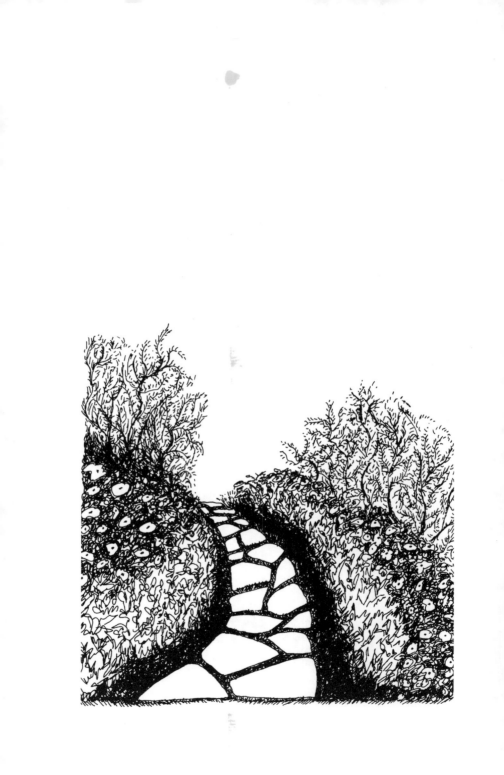

Profits from Your Backyard Herb Garden

by Lee Sturdivant

A First Steps BOOTSTRAP GUIDE

Art by Peggy Sue McRae
Photos by John Dustrude

PUBLISHED BY:
San Juan Naturals, PO Box 642, Friday Harbor, WA 98250
Printed in the United States of America.

Book design by Jack Lanning, Words & Deeds, San Jose.

ISBN 0-9621635—3-8
Library of Congress Catalog No. 95-68091

10 9 8 7 6 5 4 3 2 1

🌿 🌿 🌿 *Contents*

Preface to the Second Edition

The original version of this book, which I wrote in 1987, is out of date—particularly the parts about prices and edible flowers. And the whole subject of selling potted herbs, especially medicinal herbs, was missing entirely.

Additionally, as I've continued writing other books about small horticulture businesses that you can begin in your back yard, I've wanted to turn this original book into an even more helpful First Steps Guide, with a more thorough reference section and a few other important additions.

For years I have also wanted to change the name of this book. The first title that I chose seemed schlocky to me as soon as I saw it printed on the cover. It looked a little like: "Get Rich Quick Growing Herbs." Yuk! Not exactly what I intended.

Over the years I have come to terms with the title—primarily, I suppose, because it says what the book is really about, and because no one has accused me of not delivering on the title. To my pleasant surprise, I've actually had bunches of letters and calls from readers who have used the book with real success, and their successes have added to my own confidence in the original idea. Meanwhile, small home-based businesses grow ever more important in the American economy as more and more people seek new paths to earning their livelihood. Now that I have this opportunity to give the book a new title, I've decided to stay with the old one. After all, what I said in the beginning is still true: you can make profits from your backyard herb garden. Read on and I'll show you how.

🌿 🌿 🌿 *From Your Garden to the World of Herbs*

Fresh cut green herbs have arrived in the American kitchen, and they aren't going to go away. Herbs are also reappearing in the American medicine cabinet and those herbs, too, are only going to become more in demand.

If you're a backyard gardener, you can play a small but profitable part in these changes in our daily food and home medicine habits. This book is written to help you turn your home gardening efforts into a paying operation in the fresh herb renaissance.

We're **not** talking about get rich quick schemes. We're not talking about million dollar pay-offs. But you'll finish this book knowing exactly how to earn fifty to three or four hundred dollars a week in your spare time from your back yard. You'll be learning about growing and harvesting cut culinary herbs, and also about how to start a small herb nursery in your back yard featuring culinary, medicinal and fragrant herbs.

🌿 🌿 🌿

Just tracing the edges of the herbal renaissance in America in the past fifty years can give you some big hints about why a small herbal business can pay off. Herbs were important crops in early America, both on the dinner table and in the medicine cabinet. Then, following the industrial revolution, we threw out the past with the bath water and started all over with only the **new!** and the **scientific!**

We laughed at remembrances of family outings to pick wild greens in the country, where mustard greens and dandelions were harvested by all to be taken home for cooking.

1

We snickered with contempt at family tales of old herbal remedies as we marched off to our doctors' offices with upper arms raised for injections of the latest miracle medicines—those silver bullets that would cure us of anything and everything.

And we shook our heads in wonder at the pages of *National Geographic* showing all those savages and ignoramuses in the undeveloped world who still believed in and practiced both medicine and rituals based on the plants that grew in their area. Poor dopes, we thought, will they ever wise up and get as smart as we are? Well, look who's been wising up these days.

Following World War II we took dried herbs back into our kitchens in imitation of the Europeans, and thereby began our recent love affair with foods from all over the globe, most of which require new (to us) herbs for flavoring. The fresh culinary herb revolution in America has been led by cilantro in salsa, which is now the most popular condiment in America (surpassing even ketchup!) and that wondrous flavor of fresh basil blended with oil, garlic, nuts and cheese that we all celebrate as pesto.

The culinary rediscovery of fresh green herbs now makes our food taste better both at home and in restaurants. Kitchen herbs are also being promoted to us daily by strong forces that are reflected in the marketplace.

1. **The Gourmet Push:** Pick up any food or household magazine and recipe after recipe extols the good taste virtue of fresh cut herbs—with one luscious looking photo after another showing herbs in sauces, herbs in pastas, herbs as garnish, herbs as featured ingredients. For the gourmet, fresh herbs are in, and going to stay that way.

2. **The Salt-Free Push:** All the health and fitness magazines, newspaper columns and TV shows advocate the use of fresh and dried herbs in place of salt, now seen as an overused, even dangerous additive that we need to limit in our diets.

3. **The Simplicity Push:** This one runs right alongside (not in contrast to) the Gourmet Push. It urges us to simplify our lives and get back to basics using fewer processed foods, fresher and fresher ingredients. Fresh cut green herbs are always high on these lists, their use encouraged in place of chemical additives.

These are all very powerful forces, and they are helping to change the way we cook and serve our foods. A few years ago only the most expensive gourmet markets carried any fresh herbs besides parsley. Now produce people in markets in even the smallest towns are being asked by their customers for fresh herbs. These are the customers who are reading the cooking magazines, watching the cooking shows, tasting all the new foods in restaurants, and then wanting to try those dishes at home. They are asking your neighborhood produce manager for more and more herbs. This first part of this book is written to help you fill that market opening as a local supplier of fresh cut herbs to both markets and restaurants.

𝒲 𝒲 𝒲

Along with these culinary changes there is also the now obvious growing popularity of the use of herbs as home medicine in America. Popular over-the-counter medications are being replaced in many homes by more natural herbal preparations, either commercially produced or home prepared. This use of herbal medicine, along with other alternative (not yet mainstream) medical treatments, is starting to sweep the country. Surveys show that at least a third of Americans seek out such alternate methods in their own health care, and that percentage is increasing every year.

Plant medicine is a fascinating, complex subject, far beyond the reach of this small book, but just knowing about the increasing popularity of herbal medicine can help you in starting your backyard commercial herb endeavors. There's a fine little business to be had in growing and selling potted medicinal herbs to those who are learning to make their own medicines from home grown plants. The same can be said for growing fragrance or potpourri herbs, as these craft interests also grow more popular every year.

❧ ❧ ❧

I began selling herbs quite a few years ago, first as potted plants in farmers' markets, then wholesale to nurseries, and finally as freshly cut green herbs in the local supermarkets and restaurants. These are the same areas this beginner's book covers: first a detailed section on growing and marketing fresh cut culinary herbs, then a section on growing and marketing potted herbs, with a few business hints and recommendations in between.

❦ ❦ ❦ *Fresh Cut Culinary Herbs*

PLANNING AND GROWING

This market garden plan for cut culinary herbs is based on your having only one or two good store accounts, plus one or two fairly small restaurant accounts. If you have the room and enjoy the work, you can extend this plan almost indefinitely, but you'll soon be into something more than a small backyard operation. For those of you who have the room and interest, there will be information later leading you on to bigger things, but the primary aim here is toward the small, even the beginning market gardener.

The wonderful thing about culinary herbs in the garden is that they can be fitted in all over the yard. Plant them among both flowers and vegetables, or all by themselves. A few can even grow under trees. Most herbs prefer the sun, but a few grow well in the shade; some even do well in large planters. These are ancient plants, many are quite hardy, most of them don't require much fussing over.

I'll tell you the number of plants to grow plus a little bit about the space requirements of each herb. These gardening suggestions are also written on the assumption that you may already have a flower and/or vegetable garden on your property and that you don't want to give those up.

If you should be able to start these ideas in a new garden, raised beds would definitely be advisable: they are easier to care for and allow the kind of focused intensive gardening this plan aims for. Many gardening books these days have complete information on how to prepare and plant raised beds.

In order to keep the start-up costs down, and to encourage even small space gardeners, I've kept the number of herb plants needed to a minimum. If you have the room and can afford to plant more, feel free to do so, as you'll sell all you can grow once your business is established.

My herb gardening effort has been in the cloudy Pacific Northwest, in gardening zone six, where temperatures seldom go below ten degrees and the summers are quite cool. You must, of course, adapt this plan to your own environment and weather limitations.

If you live in a severe winter climate area, you'll have a somewhat shorter season, and may even want to consider doing some greenhouse growing. I don't cover greenhouse growing in detail in this book, but again, I do make recommendations in the reference section.

If you live in zone eight or nine, you may do much of your gardening in the fall, winter and spring, leaving only a few herbs for the hottest summertime growing. Please remember that the basic information I give for each plant is for average growing conditions. You don't have to be a gardening expert to get into this business, but every bit of gardening information you learn, especially about your own area, will help you enormously.

If this is your first gardening effort, expect this business to take a year or two to get going well. If you're already growing lots of herbs, you probably just need the marketing and packaging hints to put you in business almost instantly.

🌿 🌿 🌿 *Twelve Basic Culinary Herbs*

The herbs are listed in the order of their importance for marketing. But that can be a little different for each part of the country. Even living in an ethnic neighborhood can make a difference in the popularity of some culinary herbs.

BASIL BASICS

Ocimum basilicum

Annual. Grows to 18". Plant seed indoors in early spring.
Requires dark and 70° temperature to germinate.
Germinates in five to 10 days. Plant 6" to 8" apart.
Needs full sun.

Basil

If you only have room for one herb, make it basil. If you want to know which herb to allow the most space for, make it basil. Basil is the herb that has really switched America on to herbs, and this herb has now passed the fad stage and is fast becoming a seasoning staple.

So right away make a special place in your garden plan for basil; at least 4' x 10' if you can possibly do it. The plants can be put rather close together, say 6" to 8" apart. Try to grow at least 30 plants your first year. I would make at least two plantings of basil, three or four weeks apart, so that you can harvest it until first frost. Every time I check my sales closely, I find that the packages of basil almost always sell first. I'm certain I lose a lot of sales every year just because I don't allow even more space to this popular herb.

You should plant basil seeds; buying enough plants will be too costly. Purchase common or sweet basil seeds, not any of the unusual basils (cinnamon, licorice, holy basil, etc.). You can plant the seeds out in the garden after last frost or, a much better idea, start them indoors early and put them out as the soil warms up after the last frost. (See the seed starting information later in the book.)

Big Hint: Cover basil seedlings with a plastic tunnel. Your production will be earlier and much bigger. Basil hates cool temperatures, so keep it covered until even the nights are warm in your area.

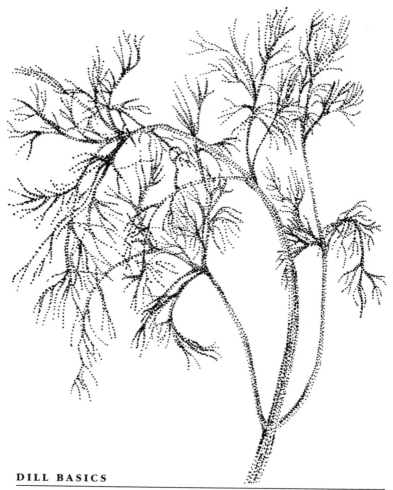

DILL BASICS

Anethum graveolens

Annual. Bouquet variety grows to 2-1/2 feet.
Plant seeds out after last frost. Soil should be 60°.
Requires light to germinate. Germination takes 14 days.
Thin plants to eight inches apart. Needs a sunny spot and
protection from the wind.

ʂ ʂ ʂ *Dill* ʂ ʂ ʂ

The first important point to be made about dill is that there are at least two types of dill seeds available and you must search out (probably by mail) the ferny or tetraploid dill seeds that are the best for a market herb garden. Ordinary dill, which grows very tall and goes to flower and seed rather quickly, is the best dill for pickling. But it is the lush ferny dill that good cooks want for salads, fish cooking and dips. If you have lots of room, it's fine to grow both kinds of dill. But find the ferny dill and start out with that. (See reference section for a list of seed houses.) Plant dill two to four times a season, depending on your sales. You need at least 20 to 30 plants each planting. Dill seedlings don't really transplant very well so it's best to plant the seeds just where you want them to grow.

FRENCH TARRAGON BASICS

Artemesia dracunculus

Hardy perennial. Cannot be grown from seed.
Grows 18" to 24" tall. Spreads. Needs sun and good drainage.
Plant starts 12" apart.

❧ *French Tarragon* ❧

Here's an herb you can't actually supply in any quantity for at least a year or two. But it's so valuable for a market herb garden that I'd like to insist that you follow along with my recommendations, put in a good tarragon bed, and I know you'll thank me later. The seeds of the French tarragon plant are sterile so you must purchase plants. (Don't bother with Russian tarragon seeds—the flavor is not the same at all.) I suggest you start with at least four plants—buy six or eight if you can afford them. Now clear a well drained sunny spot at least 3' x 6' and put your starts in as though they were little cabbage plants; about that far apart.

Tarragon plants lose their leaves in the winter; the first year you'll swear you've lost the plants. Be patient, they'll return in the spring (if they aren't allowed to sit in water during the winter). The little bed will seem to invite weeds, and tarragon and weeds are very incompatible—so keep it weeded all the time. The plants will spread, slowly but surely, and that's what they have to do before you can really start to harvest the precious leaves. I would advise against picking any leaves at all the first year (okay, one tiny taste) and that you pick rather sparingly the second year.

By the third year you'll have a strong bed that can last quite a while and pay off year after year. The plants do seem to "wear out" a bit after five or six years when you'll want to start adding new plants into the bed to help rejuvenate it, or simply dig up and divide the plants you have, which will also rejuvenate the bed.

MINT BASICS

Mentha

Start spearmint from seeds inside at 55°.
Seed germinates in 10 to 14 days. Needs light to germinate.
Plant 18" apart. Will spread.
Buy peppermint starts.
Mints are hardy perennials.

ᗰ ᗰ ᗰ *Mints* ᗰ ᗰ ᗰ

Mints take a special place in the garden because they can become so invasive. You may even want to consider planting them in large pots but, if you do, remember that mints take lots of water and can dry out very easily when grown in pots. Pot-grown mints will need watering every day in hot weather, perhaps even twice a day.

Mints can also grow in shady spots, need little care other than water and are good sellers. If you live in a mild winter area, mints can be grown all year long. I suggest you start your culinary mint beds with spearmint, which can be grown easily from seeds, and with black peppermint, which you must locate from a nursery. Peppermints seldom come true from seeds. I make a point of taking a little taste of mint wherever I come upon it and taking home starts of anything that tastes especially good. You can add other mints as you go along (apple mint, orange mint, pineapple mint, etc.) but start off with two or three good plants each of spearmint and peppermint (preferably black). Keep all mints separate from each other as they can combine and change flavor over seasons of growing into one another. Cut the plants back before they flower and they will produce a whole new crop and spread like crazy.

OREGANO BASICS

Origanum

Hardy perennial. Seeds can be started inside in winter.
Requires dark to germinate. Takes 14 days at 60° temperature.
Greek oregano grows about 10" high. Plant 18" apart.

Oregano

Most oregano seeds and nursery plants are for a purple flowered variety that grows quite easily and tastes pretty good the first year. But the best culinary variety you must try to find is the white flowered variety called Greek oregano. It has a peppery flavor that good cooks want. Start with six or eight plants of oregano set in a sunny spot. They do spread a little each year. See the reference section for places to purchase Greek oregano seeds or plants.

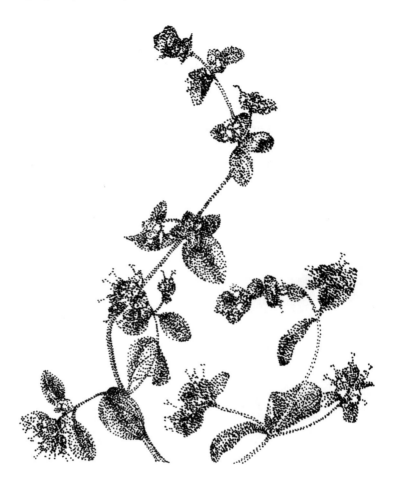

SWEET MARJORAM BASICS

Marjorana hortensis

Must be grown as an annual except in completely frost free zones. Seeds can be started inside at 60°. Needs dark to germinate. Takes 14 days. Plant in full sun 12" apart. Grows 12" to 18" tall.

Sweet Marjoram

It's important that you learn the difference between oregano and sweet marjoram, closely related but quite different culinary herbs. (Many people mix these up.) Sweet marjoram is the one with stems of knotted flowers. Oregano is the better seller in markets, is winter hardy and more well known. But sweet marjoram is a distinctively delicious herb, very popular wherever lamb is served, and is easily sold to French restaurants and other chefs.

Plant your seeds inside in winter or early spring and put them out after all frost is gone; six or eight plants will do. They must be planted every year. There is a "winter hardy" marjoram variety that herb nurseries occasionally have, but I've found it to be a little bitter. I grow new marjoram every year.

FRENCH SORREL BASICS

Rumex scutatus and *Rumex acetosa*

Hardy perennial. Grows 12" tall. Plant 12" apart. Requires ten days to germinate at 65°.

❧❧❧ *French Sorrel* ❧❧❧

Here's an herb that's growing in popularity and is quite easy to grow and take care of. Be sure to buy French Sorrel (*Rumex scutatus* or *Rumex acetosa*) seeds or plants. Start with six plants. One big problem with sorrel (which grows in partial shade) is that slugs and snails adore it. So you may have to use some bait nearby or keep after the snails and slugs every evening or early morning, when they can be seen. Sorrel sends up thick flower stalks all the time; keep these cut off to encourage more tender leaf growth.

Plant sorrel plants a foot apart; they will need dividing every couple of years. These plants do best in cool weather.

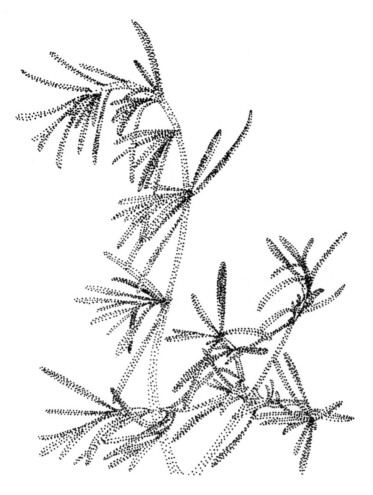

ROSEMARY BASICS

Rosemarinus officinalis

Hardy to approximately 10°. Seeds germinate slowly
(up to 21 days at 60° in the light) and sparsely
(sometimes only 10 percent). Plant in full sun and be prepared
to protect in the winter. Plant 2' to 3' apart.
Rosemary can grow up to 3' tall.

❦ ❦ ❦ *Rosemary* ❦ ❦ ❦

This is one of the few main culinary herbs that may need a little winter protection where temperatures drop below 10 or 15 degrees. I have seen rosemary plants survive below that temperature but, after losing several plants, I now give mine some winter protection. Choose carefully where to put your rosemary; give it your most protected sunny garden spot, even building a little cloche for it if necessary. In severe winter areas, grow it in pots and bring them indoors in winter. Rosemary can be started from seed, but it is so slow growing that I'd definitely recommend buying plants, three or four, to start. It will probably be quite a while before you can sell whole packets of rosemary (unless you live in a Mediterranean climate) but you can sell a very popular mix (see page 57) the first year using small bits of rosemary. There are several varieties, but stay with the standard variety (*Rosemarinus officinalis*) to start.

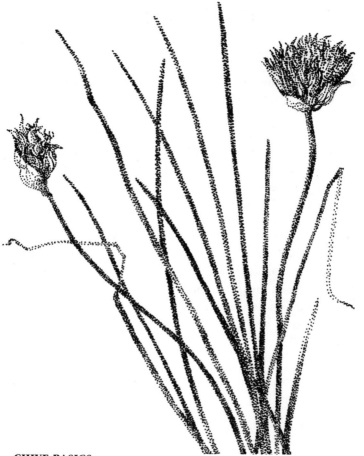

CHIVE BASICS

Allium schoenoprasum

Perennial clumps, easily grown from seed, started indoors in winter or earliest spring. Seeds take 10 days to germinate at 60°. Plants do well in sun or partial shade. Grow two feet apart and divide every year.

🌱 🌱 🌱 *Chives* 🌿 🌿 🌿

These are very easy plants to grow and you can get quite a bit of production the first year if you plant seeds early enough. Starts will give you an even faster crop; I'd suggest eight to 10 plants to start. Chives need dividing almost every year so you'll end up with quite a lot of them before long.

Chives are wonderful to grow in the flower garden, with charming (and edible) lilac flowers. Dried and freeze-dried chives taste bland compared to fresh ones. You'll find easy acceptance of your garden grown chives in both markets and restaurants.

PARSLEY BASICS

Petroselinum crispum

Hardy biennial. Soak seeds in hot water before planting. Seeds can take up to 21 days to germinate at 70°. Partial shade okay. Needs lots of moisture. Plant 8" to 10" apart.

৶ ৶ ৶ *Parsley* ৶ ৶ ৶

I'm not suggesting you supply parsley to supermarkets (although I've done a bit of that) but the mixed herb packets that sell so well (see page 57) need parsley in them and it's best to have a good supply on hand. Buy one of the very curly varieties and, if you grow it from seed (which is easily done), be patient and start early. The seeds can take up to three weeks to germinate. Cover the seed with hot water for a few minutes before planting and then plant them in pots in mid-winter and keep them warm and covered. (I give some germination hints later in the book.)

Parsley is a biennial, but you need to plant every year because last season's parsley can go to seed rather early the next season. I plant parsley seeds every mid-winter. I usually grow six to eight plants as there are so many uses for it in the kitchen.

If you keep parsley in the same place in your garden year after year, it may eventually seed itself so well you will not have to keep adding new plants. But in my garden, these natural seedlings are often less vigorous than plants from new seeds or starts.

THYME BASICS

Thymus

A perennial that is hardy in all but the most severe winters, where it must be mulched. Seeds germinate in the dark in 14 to 20 days at 70°. Plants need full sun and grow 12" high.

❧ ❧ ❧ *Thyme* ❦ ❦ ❦

There are scores of varieties of this tasty little herb, but the culinary varieties are sold as French, English or garden thyme. Any of these are fine. Some of the more exotic varieties are also good for kitchen use but you can try those later on for your own kitchen. I also get some requests for lemon thyme.

Thyme plants grow like miniature shrubs with tiny leaflets all over them and little pale flowers in summer (which the bees adore). You'll need six thyme plants in a sunny spot and they'll need replacing about every three years as they get woody. Replace one or two each year so your production won't stop.

SAGE BASICS

Salvia officinalis

A very hardy perennial, sage grows at least two feet tall. It grows from seeds or starts. Seeds germinate in 14 days at 65°. Sage requires full sun for growing.

ꙮ ꙮ ꙮ *Sage* ꙮ ꙮ ꙮ

Only one or two sage plants are necessary in your garden. It grows vigorously in a sunny spot and although not a big seller on its own, sage is a necessary addition to the Scarborough Mix, which sells very well.

I also grow several other types of sage (fruit, pineapple, silver, etc.) because the flavors are intriguing and the flowers are outstanding. I seldom sell much besides *Salvia officinalis,* and golden sage, which flowers less and keeps looking good in my garden while the regular sage is blooming. Sage can become woody and need replacing after four or five years.

Additional Possibilities 🌿 🌿 🌿

The previous twelve herbs make up my basic culinary herb business, but following is a list of other herbs and plants you may want to add to your herb garden. They can often be sold, usually in smaller amounts than the basic twelve. Perhaps some of these can become important in your area markets.

The more herbs you learn to grow and use, the more market opportunities you can find. Look over this list and try to add some of these to your garden. You can find detailed growing information about them in the many herb gardening books now on the market. I'm also including information on edible flowers, once one of my best selling items, but not quite so popular now.

Chervil

Anthriscus cerefolium. A delicious herb, but it bolts easily when the weather warms up and requires constant replanting. I swear every year that I'll give more time and patience to chervil, but I never do. A main ingredient for fines herbes.

Cilantro (Coriander Leaves)

Coriandrum sativum. An important green herb in any area where Mexican or Asian food is popular. But it takes so many plants to make up an herb packet of cilantro, and the plant itself goes so readily to seed, that I've found it to be just too much trouble to grow for market. Some years I do grow it for my own kitchen use, but many, many markets now carry it right along with parsley. See if it's readily available in your area.

Summer Savory

Satureja hortensis. This is easily grown but still not a popular green herb in my area. I do sell a little of it each season. The winter savory is even less well known. Savory is an herb you may get requests for from chefs.

Fennel

Foeniculum vulgare. I grow bronze fennel and always sell a few packets of it. Fennel is quite delicious with fish but not yet very well known or used in most areas. Some chefs will appreciate it. Green or bronze fennel is easily grown in partial shade.

Elephant Garlic

A mild yet distinctive flavor, this is actually a form of leek. I'm starting to see this garlic more and more often in markets. It's easy to grow but a little expensive to get started with. See the reference section for sources.

Garlic

I suggest you learn to grow some of this wondrous plant in your area. There are fine new books out about garlic now that can give you some real help should you decide to try to grow it in small commercial batches. See the reference section.

Shallots

If you have the extra room in your garden, shallots can be a fine addition to your sales. Grow the true French shallots; they have a rust-colored husk and a slightly purple-tinged flesh. There are several other types but these are still the most well known among good cooks.

Lovage

Levisticum officinale. One of my own personal favorites. With a strong celery taste, it makes a wonderful pesto and some chefs in my region use it constantly. Easily grown. Try to introduce it to your area.

🌿 🌿 🌿

Mixed Herbs & Greens

If your produce department has not gotten into this product yet, here is a great opportunity for a small herb grower to introduce packages of mixed greens and herbs that will be very, very popular. You'll need to grow some unusual greens: chicory, endive, oriental greens, mache, arugula, etc. Add a variety of green herb tips to the packet and customers will come back for more. Try tasting and growing some of these yourself to get the idea. Serve them with a vinaigrette. Many stores now offer these mixed greens in bulk at quite a high price. Some small farms around the country are making a success producing only this special crop. But, like much else, it may prove too competitive for its recent high price to hold up. For a small herb grower, though, it's a good product to try if your market isn't carrying this in bulk.

Edible Flowers

In the '80s, edible flowers became such a fad in restaurants (I could even sell little packets of them to home cooks) that an edible blossom was seldom safe around my house. That seems to have passed although some chefs still use them—mostly as a garnish—so I'll pass along the information I learned in those heady times of fresh flowers on every restaurant serving plate.

Probably the most important thing to learn about is the safety factor. Many blossoms can be toxic, even fatally so. The lists that follow will keep you out of trouble in that department.

EDIBLE BLOSSOMS

Borage *Borago officinalis*
Bergamot *Monarda didyma*
Calendula *Calendula officinalis*
Carnations *Dianthus*
Chrysanthemum *C. morifolium*
Citrus blossoms
Daylilies *Hemerocallis*
English daisy *Bellis Perennis*
Fuchsia
Geranium *Pelargonium*
Gladiolus
Hollyhock *Althaea rosea*
Lavender *Lavandula vera*
Lilac *Syringa*
Marigold *Tagates*
Nasturtiums *Tropaeolum majus*
Pansy and Viola *Viola hortensis, V. cornuta.*
Rose *Rosa*
Squash blossoms

TOXIC BLOSSOMS

Autumn crocus *Colchicum autumnale*
Columbine *Aquilegia vulgaris*
Foxglove *Digitalis purpurea*
Fritillaria *Fritillary meleagris*
Hydrangea *Hydrangea macrophylla*
Iris *Iris foetidissima*
Lily of the valley *Convallaria majalis*
Monkshood *Aconitum napellus*
Oleander *Nerium oleander*
Poppies *Papaver*
Rhododendron
Stonecrop *Sedum acre*
St. Johnswort *Hypericum perforatum*

🌿 🌿 🌿

The other thing to remember is that most blossoms hide tiny insects inside them. So, if you are going to prepare blossoms for marketing, be sure to take extra time to prepare them carefully: soak the blossoms for a few minutes in cold water, then allow them to dry upside down (to drain) on white paper towels. This will usually get rid of any critters. Then put the blossoms in a protective package (I buy small hard plastic food holders from the local deli), and keep in the refrigerator until used. The blossoms only keep for a very few days, at most. In my area, the price ranges from about eight cents a blossom (for pansies) to 50 cents a blossom (for squash blossoms).

🌿 🌿 🌿 Marketing Culinary Herbs

I am always amazed at how intimidated people are by the idea of marketing or selling anything they produce. They imagine there's an impossibly high wall between what goes on in the front of a grocery store and what goes on in back, where they never feel welcome.

The people who are welcome in the back of the store are the people with something good to sell. And that's what you'll have with fresh green herb packets.

What follows is a step by step method to sell your herbs after your herb garden is producing at least 4 herbs in decent quantities. Read it over several times before you start out to sell. It should help you with those first steps, which are always the hardest.

My herbs in a local market

37

After that you'll probably improve on my system and go on from there.

Pick your stores carefully. You'll want a busy store, but don't start with the big chains. (More about that later.) Look for a store with signs of being successful at what it's doing. Look over the produce section and ask yourself: Are these grocers trying hard to reach the good cooks in this area? Is there a large refrigerated produce section? This is very important, as fresh cut herbs are most like lettuce or spinach and must be constantly refrigerated to remain crisp and fresh.

Be sure to check out any food co-ops in your area, or large produce stands that have refrigeration. You only need a few stores; even one or two can sell many packets of herbs, but you want to find the best ones for your product.

You're going to be a small but high quality supplier, so it's important that you not spread yourself too thin, especially to start. Don't put your herbs in marginal stores, those that seem to be having a hard time staying open, or are really just a small addition to gasoline sales or something like that. Most convenience stores (like 7-Eleven™) don't have real produce sections; they are not good ones to choose.

After you've chosen a market, look to see if they are already selling fresh herbs. If they are, find out if the herbs are supplied locally. Usually the herbs will be labeled showing where they come from. If they are local and there's a good selection, move on to another store for your first account. It's best to start your business with all the advantages, and trying to displace someone who's already doing a good job is not an advantage. But if the herbs are from hundreds or thousands of miles away, you can offer the store real savings if they switch to your herbs.

So now you have picked out your first target store. Then you must find out the produce buyer's name and the hours during which he or she can be seen. You can get that information at the store or from home on the phone. Make an early morning appointment to see the buyer to show him "a locally grown product I know you'll like." Then prepare at least two or three packets of your garden fresh herbs to show (see the chapter on harvesting and preparation). It's a thousand times better to take in fresh herb packets than to just go in and talk about them. Most buyers get too many people coming in to tell what they can do IF the buyer will promise to buy a lot. Showing your well presented herbs is the very best way to get an order.

THE SPIEL

Here's what your greengrocer is most interested in when considering a new product: Having a good selection of products to keep the customers coming in, and making a decent profit on them without a big loss in unsold waste. You can now offer the greengrocer all of the above.

"I grow these kitchen herbs in my back yard. I'm prepared to keep you supplied in fresh culinary herbs, take back any packets that don't sell, and try to meet any special needs your customers might have. I get $1.25 for each packet that sells. Most stores sell them for $1.79 to $1.99 per packet. I can bill you weekly or monthly. I'll check the display at least twice a week. I'm reliable and eager to make my little herb business grow."

That's the basic information you need to get across. Read it over and over until you know exactly what to say. Be straightforward and good humored and don't waste time with small talk. You'll have a chance to get acquainted later as you do business there. Produce people are very, very busy in the best markets and expect you to be businesslike in your dealings with them.

This basic spiel is all the selling you have to do to get into the herb business. If you've chosen the right market, you'll find that getting the account is not a problem. Produce people these days know that herbs are becoming big business because their customers are asking for them.

Now let's take a look at just what you've offered and are asking for in return.

First of all, you're not asking for an order for so many packets of such and such an herb. That's not the best way for a backyard grower to market herbs. You want to keep as much control as possible in this little business and that means being able to sell just what you have that's ready to harvest. In most weather zones you can supply some herbs from May to October, but not all varieties that whole time. In some zones you can supply almost all year-round. These days your sales will always be highest during the basil season, but other herbs, like dill and tarragon for instance, are becoming very, very popular, too.

What you're really wanting is to rent a tiny space on your greengrocer's refrigerated counter where you can keep the market supplied with something they and their customers want. By offering to take back any packets that don't sell, you can also control your sales because you'll know exactly what to offer and can monitor the sales very well. Often grocers can order the "wrong" items, then when they don't sell, the grocer takes the loss and the supplier doesn't get any more business. You can take the first losses, learn from your customers and continue to supply what they want. This point is very important. You want to decide just what to bring into the market.

As far as your price is concerned, this business is worth doing at $1.25 to $1.35 per packet. The approximately 50 or 60 per cent mark-up the grocer then takes is quite generous but your grocer is free to mark it up higher if he wants to—he knows what his customers will pay. The fee to you should remain steady. That's what makes all the work worthwhile. (For information on weights and amounts, see the chapter on harvesting and preparation.)

So now you have your first good account. Before you go dashing off to sell to Store Number Two, take time to learn how to service Store Number One, and turn it into a good paying account. Here are some suggestions to follow in taking care of that first store.

After the grocer agrees to try your herbs:

1. Take in at least 15 or 20 packets for your first delivery.
2. Take your first order in a nice basket. In case the store doesn't have a small tray for the refrigerated counter, you can leave the

basket. Herbs look great in a basket and sell very well from one. **Just be sure it stays in the refrigerated section.**

3. Take along a small sign, "Local Fresh Herbs." You can attach it to the basket or the display until the market gets around to making its own. Make your sign as waterproof as possible as water sprays are often used over the whole refrigerated section.

4. Offer to price your own packets. Sometimes a store will appreciate the help in marking; other stores will just have you leave the herbs in the back until an employee has time to mark them.

5. Be certain to have an employee sign for each delivery. (See the business details section for more on this.)

6. To start with, keep a separate tally of which herbs you take in so that you can learn what's selling the fastest. Bring in not less than six packets of herbs per delivery. Remove any packets that start looking unappetizing. If the herbs are packaged correctly and kept in the refrigerated section, they should hold up fine for about a week—some for longer.

Don't get discouraged if the sales are slow to start. Customers have to get to used to seeing a new vegetable or fruit or greens. You may even lose money for the first few weeks, but if you've chosen the right store and grown fine herbs, you'll soon start selling lots of packets and decide it's time to look for a second account. Be certain your garden will produce enough now to more than double your sales. It may be you'll want to stay with just one market the first season, until your garden is producing more.

Now, what about those chain stores? Yes, definitely consider them, especially if there are no good locally owned stores in your area. But your sales method may have to be quite different. Many, but not all, large chains forbid their produce managers to buy local crops. Your produce manager will tell you this when you go in to see him. But show him your packets and ask if he'd like to carry them if you go to the trouble of going to the main office. If he's interested, it may be worth your while to go further. Those buying offices may be a long way away, even a hundred miles or so. I've never felt the additional expense would be worth it. I have always found that it's easier to look harder for small specialty stores, delis, or locally owned groceries. While your first herb crops are growing, take your time to find just the right first account. Here are some hints on improving sales in the store account once you have it.

IMPROVING YOUR SALES

Be certain that during the time you are learning how to grow and sell culinary herbs you are also learning to use them in your own home kitchen. You will be asked endless questions about cooking with herbs as you become involved in their selling; make sure you learn enough about their use to speak intelligently and give recommendations to consumers eager to try these new flavors in their recipes.

I recommend several herb cookbooks in the bibliography, and offer at least one recipe per herb in the harvesting chapter. I want to encourage you to work with herbs in your kitchen every day. You will become more enthusiastic about these magical green plants as you use them.

One of the very best ways to improve your market sales is to arrange to do a food demonstration at the market that sells your herbs. This is an easy way to increase your sales for the short term and also familiarize the customers with the taste of fresh herbs.

To give a food demonstration in your market, you agree on a day and time with the produce manager (usually a Friday or Saturday afternoon when the market is certain to be busy) and you set up a small table covered with a colorful tablecloth, near the produce department. One very easy and good tasting tidbit for an herb demonstration is herb-cheese stuffed celery bites. Blend chopped green herbs with low-fat cottage cheese or yogurt and then stuff tiny bits of celery and serve from a plate in the market. The celery is bland enough to let the herb flavor come through and makes a fine little holder. You can also use crackers.

You need to experiment a little with this at home to get something you like and that you know will taste good to others. Use tarragon, basil, chives or oregano—herbs you have in quantity, as you'll sell a lot of those.

Food demonstrations are a wonderful way for you to learn about your customers; they will engage you in endless conversations (keep giving out samples to other customers as you chat). Take along some tiny paper napkins, a waste basket, a plate for serving, a cutting board and knife. Make up the cheese blend at home. The market will sell or give you the celery and a place to wash and cut it up. Cut up a lot before you start, stash it in a plastic bag and put it in the store's refrigerator section until you need it.

A store may expect a discount on the product you sell that day—say, $1.00 to you for a packet for that one day only. They will likely mark down the herb price to the customer, too. I'd agree to all this, but only if asked. Don't volunteer to give anything away.

Another way to increase sales in markets is to supply little herb recipe cards near your display. Type your favorite herb recipe (be sure you have plenty of that herb on hand) on an 8-1/2" x 11" sheet, making six or eight copies of the recipe on the one sheet. Make 10 or 12 copies of the sheet and then cut out the recipes with a paper cutter (or scissors). Finally, staple the stack of 20 to 30 recipes to a cardboard backing and take them to the greengrocer to put up near your herbs. Again, make sure you do this when you have a lot of the herb on hand that you're featuring in the recipe. Feel free to use my recipes. And, again, watch out for the water sprays, so the recipe cards don't get spoiled.

MARKETING CULINARY HERBS TO RESTAURANTS

Restaurants are a golden opportunity for a backyard herb dealer. Pick out the gourmet restaurants in your area or, more to the point, those restaurants that feature lots of fresh vegetables, specialty salads, homemade soups and breads. By phone you can find out the name of the chef and what time she comes to work. Try to see the chef as early in the day as possible. Like the greengrocer, chefs are very busy people. Use the same spiel you do for markets, but of course chefs won't be reselling your packets directly. Take in two or three packets to start, keep your price at $1.25 or $1.35, leave the packets with her to try (no charge) and call back in a day or two to see if you can do business there. You may find that one or two restaurants plus one good market account can use up your fresh herb supply quite nicely, especially the first year or two.

Let your contact with chefs encourage your own efforts in learning ever more about culinary herb use in your own kitchen. As your abilities with culinary herbs grow stronger, you will find ever more common ground with the chefs and will be able to make suggestions, take in new samples for them to try, encourage more experimentation on their part. Many restaurants are now even beginning to feature wildcrafted herbs: herbs such as nettles and dandelions collected from the wild. Your own little culinary herb business can also lead you in these directions. Some herb growers become wildcrafters, too.

After your garden is well established and you know just what to expect from your plants (and have probably added to your inventory based on your own sales) you can reach out to all sorts of new accounts.

Make friends at the delis and restaurants you think might be interested in using your fresh herbs. I once supplied a recipe and a sample bowl of sorrel soup to the owner of a small restaurant who seemed anxious to serve very fresh food and please her customers. The owner was delighted and served sorrel soup for months using my sorrel. Give restaurant owners and chefs new herbs to try. Make suggestions.

Who teaches cooking classes in your area? They will be interested in using your product and in telling their students where to get your herbs.

You can sell packets of fresh herb packets at a farmers' market. On hot days, be sure to take along a tub of ice to display them in (out of the sun!) and don't undercut yourself if your market account is nearby. If your market account is quite some distance away, sell your herbs at the farmers' market for one dollar to one fifty a packet. When you have lots of basil, dill and French tarragon, you can make many sales.

These are just a few of the ideas I have used over the years to increase my own sales. I hope they'll lead you to even better ideas for your growing business.

🌿 🌿 🌿

I also sell herbs through a fruit and vegetable distributor who deals only with restaurants. He took around packets of my herbs to his accounts and now calls in his orders to me once or twice a week. You can learn the names of the distributors in your area from the chefs you sell to, but please be careful about getting over-extended for your first year or two. The growing season is rather short, and there is really quite a bit of work to do when you begin. You want to get a reputation as a reliable, high quality herb grower, so don't go tearing around over-selling, and then be unable to deliver. It's far better to be small the first year or two while you are learning this business, and then determine how big you should get after you know exactly what's involved for your own life. Learning just what your plants will produce takes at least a year of cautious observation before deciding you can supply everyone who wants your herbs.

Harvesting, Packaging and Kitchen Use

Perhaps you've noticed in the sales section of this book that I never mention herb packet weights. If you've already started looking at herbs in markets, you've seen that many herbs are sold by weight. Some are sold by the small bundle. When I started in this business, I wanted to get into it without a lot of start-up costs. I wanted to make sure there really was a good market out there for my herbs before investing in such costly things as commercial scales and fancy printed labels. That conservative system worked so well that I still don't use scales, although I did invest in printed labels for my herb packets near the end of my second year.

What worked for me can work for you in this low cost way to start your own herb business.

PACKAGE and LABEL

When you first decide to go into business, you'll need to choose a company name and have a little rubber stamp made with that name, your address and phone number on it. That will come in handy both with your billing and with making labels.

For packaging, purchase a package of plastic freezer bags at your supermarket. As of this writing, my local store sells 80 one-quart capacity bags for about two dollars. They measure 4"x2"x12" and are .95 mil thick. Then purchase a small package of stick-on labels measuring approximately 2"x3" or 3"x4". There are many sizes available. As of this writing, these are for sale at my local drug store for approximately four dollars for a package of 150 bags.

47

The next thing you'll need is a waterproof pen. A laundry pen will work quite well. These few items are the basic packaging you'll need the first season. It will keep your costs at a few pennies per pack.

Now all you need to add is a little bit of creative thinking about making your first labels by hand. Or maybe you're like me and panic at the thought of drawing so much as a flower petal. If so, just consider using a rubber stamp. You're going to need one anyway for billing.

Your label should say: FRESH HERBS, Company Name, Telephone Number and Address. Be sure to leave lots of white space on the label where you can write in with a waterproof pen the name of the herb.

The address and phone number give customers a chance to reach you and that kind of identification is usually necessary under the law. Make your labels and stick them onto the bags just before you harvest. Write the herb name on the label before you fill the bag. **Be sure to use a waterproof pen.**

I'm including a picture of my own herb label to give you an idea when you do go to printed labels. But I would advise against printed labels the first year. Good herbs will sell easily with hand-made labels and you should concentrate your first year on learning the business and taking money in. Spending money is easy. Learn the fun of going into your local markets to sell them something instead of always buying. I'm also including a picture of a hand-made label like the one I used the first year.

ℓ ℓ ℓ

The label I now use in my herb packets is known as a "crack & peel" label, and is quickly applied, easily stored and looks good in the produce market. The ink is dark purple. The one problem with these labels is the expense: up to ten cents each in quantities of less than a thousand or so. That's why I don't recommend them for beginning herb growers. Keep your expenses as low as possible the first year while you make sure this little business is

Oregano

SAN JUAN NATURALS
BOX 642
FRIDAY HARBOR, WA 98250

☙ **FRESH HERBS** ☙
Organically Grown in Friday Harbor

Oregano

When flavor matters, use fresh, green herbs in your favorite recipes.
Keep this packet well-chilled in your refrigerator, as you would salad greens. Wash and dry the herbs just before use.
When a recipe calls for ½ t. of dried herbs, try using 3 or 4 tspns. chopped fresh herbs.
Adjust to taste
For fullest flavor add herbs the last few minutes of cooking just before serving.
Unused herbs may be saved by drying at room temperature.

SAN JUAN NATURALS
Box 642
Friday Harbor, WA 98250
378-2648

The plain label can also be jazzed up with rubber stamps, stickers, or art work. The printed label is called "crack and peel." Be sure to use a waterproof pen on both kinds of labels.

49

the right one for you. Make your first labels by hand, or with a rubber stamp. Printed labels can come later.

HOW and HOW MUCH TO PICK

So now your first crop of herbs is ready to be harvested and taken to the greengrocer. What follows is an herb by herb description of harvesting and packaging for market. Because we're not using a scale, some of the descriptions of how much to pick may seem a little vague. You must always look at what you're doing with one eye for the customer. Is the person who buys your little herb packet going to feel that they are getting good value for their money? By now you will have checked out several markets where herbs are sold and know if you're giving good value in comparison to those herb bundles. When herbs are growing well, they produce lots and lots of pickable harvest. Be generous in your packaging and you'll never hear any complaints. If you're too skimpy your sales will drop off.

The time of day you pick your herbs is not as important as the fact that they are dry when you pick them. Wet herbs rot quickly in the plastic bags, so time your watering for after harvest. Don't wash your herbs before selling for the same reason. I grow herbs without using herbicides or pesticides on or around them, so I'm not worried about the produce I take to market. I strongly suggest you follow that pattern, too.

But what if, you might ask, you go to the garden and find the lovely dill fronds covered with aphids? Well, it can certainly happen, and since I'm strongly advising against the use of pesticides, I had better give you some solution for such a problem at harvest time. Of course you'd wash off the aphids, carefully and gently in cold water. I'd also urge the use of a salad spinner to dry the herbs after that washing. Even blotting with paper towels is a good idea in order to take the herbs to market dry, so they'll last longer. Incidentally, I never seal the plastic bags, but leave them open at the top. The smell of fresh cut herbs is a big selling point; with open bags customers can sniff all they like, or even taste.

If you pick in the heat of the day, don't leave the filled bags in the sun. Place them in your refrigerator until you finish picking the whole order and can take them to market. On hot days, you can take a bucket of ice to the garden. It's very important to keep the herbs cold, and out of the sun.

I use my fingers and fingernails to pinch off the stem ends of almost all herbs, but a small knife or pair of scissors is needed for cutting chive bunches. I kneel on a plastic pad at each plant I'm harvesting and can easily pick 30 or 40 mixed bags of herbs in less than an hour. You'll be slower, of course, to start, but that's mostly because you'll be uncertain of how much to pick.

When you're first learning to package, get hold of a little postage (oz.) scale. (Anyone who has ever belonged to Weight Watchers™ should have one.) I'll give you some approximate weights to start, but the most important point to ask yourself is: How does the bag look? Am I giving good value?

Also remember that, for gardeners, brown spots on leaves or even slightly chewed leaves come to look nearly perfect to us. Sadly, these tiny blemishes will stop many retail customers right in their tracks. They are not used to the imperfect; they seem almost trained to hate imperfections. To gain such people as customers you must keep everything looking as nearly perfect as possible. When the whole country finally takes up gardening, everything will surely be much saner and more realistic. Meanwhile, make it all look as perfect as possible.

I am also including some recipe information in this section to try again to push you into using more herbs in your own kitchen. That will lead you to more ideas for sales, more enthusiasm for what you are doing. When you get the habit of fresh green herbs for the kitchen, you'll find yourself preparing food as usual, getting ready to serve it, and suddenly remembering that you can make it taste so much better if you just go out to the garden and pinch off a few fresh green herbs to add at the last moment of cooking. I keep a wooden planter of herbs at the kitchen door for just such a quick fix. It takes only a moment, and makes a big difference in taste.

🌿🌿🌿 Harvesting Hints and Herb Use in the Kitchen

BASIL HARVESTING

The first thing to remember about harvesting this herb is to not let it go to flower. Flower and seed setting on a basil plant stops its leaf production and spoils the plant for harvesting. If flower stems appear, pick them immediately and include them in your packet for market. A lot of basil is sold by the uprooted bunch, but I prefer to nurse my plants along, picking leaves and stems carefully so that the same plants will produce for me from mid-June through September or even October. I make at least two plantings, but I don't abandon the first one when the second is ready to pick. I just go back and forth, one bed to another, letting the plants rest between pickings. Ten to 15 basil stems (depending on the leaf size) should make a full looking bag and weigh in at about 2 ounces. (All these weights are very approximate, and depend on the size and maturity of the leaves and stems. Your eyes are the best judge of good value.)

BASIL IN THE KITCHEN

This key herb is nearly synonymous with the word pesto, which itself derives from the word pestle. Although many different herbs

---

BASIL PESTO

Put one to two cups of basil leaves in a blender or food processor. Add two to four cloves of garlic, 1/2 to a full cup of parsley leaves. Blend and chop thoroughly, and then slowly add 3/4 cup good olive oil. Also add 1/2 cup grated Parmesan cheese and 1/4 cup pine nuts or walnuts. (The nuts are optional.) Blend all into a thick sauce. This sauce is perfect over any cooked pasta or noodles. It is a fine addition (a tablespoon at a time) to any salad dressing; a tasty spread for sliced tomatoes; a super sandwich if you add Italian cheese and French bread. Indeed, basil pesto can be used to flavor any vegetable, baste any barbecue, or be used any time great flavor is needed. Just make it and taste—you'll think of new ways to use it yourself.

---

can be used to make delicious herb pastes (pestos) the most common is made with a recipe similar to the one opposite.

DILL HARVESTING

Here's another reminder to be sure you're growing the ferny or tetraploid dill. Ten or 12 stems of mature ferny dill should weigh in at about 1-1/2 ounces and make a fine looking package. When the plants are quite young, perhaps 12 or 15 stems will be needed. Just make the package look good to a cook, who can dry any extra dill not needed immediately. It will keep well for quite a while in the refrigerator.

DILL IN THE KITCHEN

Fresh green dill leaves can be used in place of dill seeds in almost any recipe. Dill is extra nice for use in salads, in yogurt or sour cream dips, and in the cooking of fish, especially salmon.

DILL MAYONNAISE SALMON

Put salmon filets or steaks on a cookie sheet and cover the top with dill fronds. Spread a mixture of mayonnaise and dijon mustard over the fish. (Use one large tablespoon of mustard for each 1/2 cup mayo.)
Broil the fish about three inches from the heat until fish flakes easily with a fork.

FRENCH TARRAGON HARVESTING

It takes almost half the season in my area for the tarragon bed to really produce well, so I only sell a few bags a week until early July. Then I sell as much tarragon as possible to markets and restaurants while it's at the peak of production. Ten to 12 stems will make a good looking bag and should weigh about 1-1/2 ounces.

FRENCH TARRAGON IN THE KITCHEN

What a tasty, anise-like addition to so many dishes. Excellent with chicken, eggs and fish, tarragon is also a savory seasoning for potatoes, spinach, peas and cauliflower.

TARRAGON CHICKEN SALAD

2 cups diced cold chicken
1 cup finely chopped celery
1 cup green grapes cut in half
3/4 cup low-fat mayonnaise
1 or 2 tablespoons chopped tarragon

Combine all ingredients and mix gently but thoroughly. Let stand one hour in the refrigerator before serving. Non-fat yogurt can be substituted.

Tarragon bed in early summer

THE SCARBOROUGH MIX

This herb mix often outsells all but basil in my market accounts, and I seriously recommend it to you. It's a fine way to gain new customers who can try several herbs at once. It also makes a good herb mix at home chopped in salads, soups, etc. In the bottom of the plastic bag, place five or six fluffy sprigs of curly parsley, then add three or four stems of sage, three or four stems of thyme leaves (and flowers) and two or three stems of rosemary. Mark the label: Parsley, Sage, Rosemary and Thyme and, if you're generous with your parsley, it will be a lovely, fragrant packet of useful herbs that many people will buy.

MINT HARVESTING

I probably fill my mint bags fuller than any others because mint is occasionally for sale rather cheaply and I want my customers to feel they're getting a big bag full of mint from me. I only use stem ends with perfect leaves (not snail eaten or moldy) and I fill the bag almost to the top. Try 15 or even 20 stems and the bag might weigh 2 or more ounces. I often use mixed mint varieties and mark the bag MINTS.

MINTS IN THE KITCHEN

Too often seen as a mere garnish for iced tea, fresh mint can easily become a basic herb in your kitchen. Here are a couple of ideas to get you started taking mint a little more seriously in your own kitchen.

ZUCCHINI WITH MINT

Grate or finely chop 6 or 8 small zucchini and sauté in 2 tablespoons melted butter. Add 1/4 cup chopped spearmint or peppermint and sauté for a minute or two. Salt and pepper to taste. Serves 3 or 4.

GARBANZO SPINACH SALAD

1 large or 2 small heads spinach
1 16 oz. can garbanzo beans
1 cup diced celery
1/2 cup raisins
1/4 cup chopped mint leaves

Wash, dry and chop spinach . Add washed, drained garbanzo beans, celery, raisins and chopped mint. Dress with vinaigrette. Serves 4 to 6.

Oregano harvesting can be done easily by thumb and forefinger, or by using small scissors.

OREGANO HARVESTING

This can be a little tedious to pick as Greek oregano is somewhat smaller and slower growing than the more common variety. But the Greek variety is appreciated by cooks, so I do strongly recommend it. In harvesting, try 12 to 15 stem ends weighing approximately 1-1/2 ounces. Add a few flower stems and blossoms, if there are any.

MARJORAM HARVESTING

It can be harvested much as the oregano, and weighs about the same. When the knotted flower stems start blooming, add a few stems to each packet for fragrance, looks and taste.

OREGANO AND MARJORAM IN THE KITCHEN

These herbs can be used interchangeably and together.

SIMPLE SPAGHETTI OR PASTA SAUCE ₪ ₪ ₪

4 cups chopped fresh tomatoes
1 cup chopped onion
2 tablespoons olive oil
3 tablespoons chopped oregano leaves
2 tablespoons chopped marjoram leaves
Salt to taste

Put all ingredients together in a saucepan and simmer 20 to 30 minutes. Serve over pasta with grated Parmesan cheese. Add a few more chopped green leaves with the cheese.

HERB BUTTER ₪ ₪ ₪

A delicious seasoning for French bread.
1/2 cup sweet butter
1/4 cup finely chopped marjoram, oregano and basil leaves

Whip together in a food processor or blender. Spread on sliced French bread before or after heating, or at the table. For extra flavor, add 1 or 2 cloves garlic.

FRENCH SORREL HARVESTING

As your sorrel bed develops, you'll have small, medium and large leaves. The largest leaves may need folding to fit in the bag. Once a plant gets overgrown with very large leaves, I cut it back completely so that new, more tender leaves will grow. The flavor is often better from smaller leaves. Don't include stems in your

Fresh sorrel leaves after cutting tall stems

sorrel bags; they are not edible and take up too much space. I fill a sorrel bag completely, much as I do for mint. A full bag of sorrel may weigh as much as three ounces or more. As I have mentioned before, the important thing to remember with sorrel is to keep the seed stalks cut back as soon as they appear.

FRENCH SORREL IN THE KITCHEN

For an easy beginning with this distinctive herb, try some sorrel leaves in your next tuna salad—maybe one fourth as much sorrel as lettuce. Then try sorrel leaves chopped into your next cole slaw. Sorrel has the ability to make ordinary foods taste a little bit extraordinary.

SORREL SOUP

2 tablespoons butter
2 or 3 medium potatoes
2 cups washed, chopped sorrel
1 cup chopped onion
3 cups chicken stock
1 cup low fat milk

Sauté the onions until quite wilted, then add the chopped sorrel and sauté another minute or two. Meanwhile, wash, peel and slice the potatoes. Add them to the pan with the onions plus the chicken stock. Bring to a boil and simmer for 25 or 30 minutes until the potatoes are tender. Put through a blender or processor. Return to the pan. Stir in milk and reheat if you are serving the soup hot, or chill it to serve cold. Do not bring it to a boil after adding milk.

ROSEMARY HARVESTING

At least six or eight stems of rosemary are needed per bag when you're selling rosemary by itself. The weight would be approximately one ounce. But it's a slow growing plant in most weather zones, so you may not have a big supply of rosemary to offer your first year. In fact, it might be a good idea to use it exclusively the first year in the Scarborough Mix. If you live in a very warm sunny climate, you can sell heaps of it all the time.

ROSEMARY IN THE KITCHEN

OVEN FRIES WITH ROSEMARY

Cut three baking potatoes into 8 wedges each. Place potatoes in an oiled oven-proof dish and pour 1/4 cup good olive oil over all. Then sprinkle with 2 tablespoons chopped rosemary. Cover the dish and cook for about 20 minutes at 350°. Remove from oven, uncover, turn the potatoes, turn up the oven to 425° and cook for another 10 minutes or so until the potatoes are golden brown and quite tender. The outside should be a little crispy. Cook them until they are. Serves 4 or 5.

BEETS WITH ROSEMARY

This can be made with fresh or canned beets, as fresh herbs can jazz up even the most mundane of foods. Cook and slice fresh beets, or open a can of sliced beets. Drain the liquid into a saucepan (or save the cooking liquid.) Add 1/2 cup any flavorful vinegar, 1/4 cup sugar and three rosemary sprigs cut from the branch tips. Boil for a few minutes and then pour over the beets in a bowl. Chill before serving.

Chive harvesting

CHIVE HARVESTING

When harvesting chives, even for your own use, be certain to cut them off close to the bottom of the plant instead of snipping at the tip ends of the plants. Circle a bunch of chives, about three inches in diameter, with your left hand and, holding them firmly, cut through the greens an inch from the ground. For the first cutting or two, the chives will be clean and ready to place in the plastic bag. However, after a few harvests they become "dirty" with weeds and stiff flower stems, etc. When you cut these "dirtier" chives you should then hold the cut bunch close to the tips and shake them. All the junk will drop out. Trim off any yellow tips (from previous cuttings) and make the chives look as perfect as possible. The packet weight should be about three ounces. If available, it's nice to include a stem or two of chive buds or flowers in each packet.

Chive flowers are edible fresh in salads and are delicious dipped in tempura batter and fried. This is handy when you end up with as many chive plants as I do.

CHIVES IN THE KITCHEN

There's no way to use up all the chives you're going to be growing; just remember to add them chopped to soup, salad, vegetables or omelets. They are perfect, of course, for chive butter or in sour cream. Eight or 10 chive stems chopped up into a tuna salad will quickly lift the flavor.

CHIVE BLOSSOMS IN TEMPURA BATTER 🌿 🌿 🌿

Wash chive blossoms gently but thoroughly.
(Tiny insects love to hide in all flower blossoms.)
Dry the blossoms by use of a salad spinner or by shaking dry in a colander. Buy dry tempura batter or make it with 1 cup cake flour, 1 cup ice water, 1 egg, 1/4 teaspoon baking powder and 1/4 teaspoon salt. Stir gently, then add another 1/3 cup (approx.) cake flour to blend in with only one or two strokes. Set the batter bowl in ice water as you're working. The batter will be lumpy.
Dip the washed, dry chive blossoms in the batter, three or four at a time, and fry in peanut oil at 375° for about two minutes—or until golden brown.
Use a wok if you have one. Drain well.

Harvest thyme stems, leaves, flower buds and blossoms.

THYME HARVESTING

It can take a few stems of thyme to make a decent package, perhaps eight or nine multi-stemmed sprigs. I also usually include a few thyme flowers. They are pretty, edible and add to the look of the packet. The approximate weight of a thyme packet might be one ounce. I don't cut and package woody stems. Only the tender green stems are edible.

THYME IN THE KITCHEN

The most common use of fresh thyme is in bouquets garnis (tied-up herbs to season soups and stocks) or as a key ingredient in clam chowder. Actually, used in moderation, thyme leaves can add zip to all sorts of soups and salads or any long, slow-cooked meat dish. I also like the flavor in sautéed or braised onions.

SAUTÉED ONIONS WITH THYME

Slice one pound of onions while melting 2 or 3 tablespoons of unsalted butter in a pan. If the thyme is tender stemmed, add 2 tablespoons finely chopped leaves and stems. If the stems are woody, roll the stems between your hands to strip off the tiny flavorful leaves. Let the thyme cook for two or three minutes in the butter, then add the sliced onions, stir and cook for at least 20 or 30 minutes until the onions start to brown. This is a wonderful side dish to go with roasted or barbecued meats. It also makes a fine pizza topping.

SAGE HARVESTING

Although used primarily in the Scarborough Mix, a few packets of sage do sell, especially during winter holidays. Try 12 to 15 tip ends in a packet and add a flower stem or two when available. The packet should weigh about 1-1/2 ounces. I must stress one last time that you let your eye be your guide on this harvesting. Try to deliver packets that look both perfect (no brownish tips, no bits of weed or dirt) and very generous. Follow these two rules and you will be successful, no matter what your packets weigh.

SAGE IN THE KITCHEN

It almost seems worth growing a sage plant just to have it for Thanksgiving dressing and to garnish the turkey platter. But there are some other uses you may like; it is very good in bread, corn bread and biscuits. Give these biscuits a try and see what you think.

SAGE BISCUITS 🌿 🌿 🌿

2 cups flour
3 teaspoons baking powder
1 teaspoon salt
2 tablespoons finely minced sage leaves
1/3 cup oil
2/3 cup milk

Mix the dry ingredients in a bowl, make a hole in the center and add the liquid. Stir only until well mixed. Drop by heaping tablespoons onto a greased cookie sheet and bake in a preheated 450° oven for 10 or 12 minutes until the tops are lightly browned.

🌿 🌿 🌿 *Getting into Business*

What follows are a few concerns that will apply both to a fresh cut culinary herb business and also to a potted herb business, the details of which are in the following section.

Do you live in a town or county that requires a business license? Does your state require you to have a resale number in order to do business? Will you have a zoning problem if you grow commercial crops in your garden?

If you've never been in business, all these questions may seem very serious and difficult—like obstacles in your way. But there are a couple of things to remember here before you get too worried over "the legalities."

1. The tax laws, and most other laws, can actually favor small businesses. All the red tape you hear and read so much about primarily concerns large and medium size businesses—those businesses that the government is trying to keep track of and work with on one thing and another. The business we are talking about is so small as to be nearly invisible: small and straightforward. You won't have a lot of red tape to deal with.
2. Retail business people often collect sales taxes for their state, county and/or town. These are called retail sales taxes. If your state has a retail tax system (and all but few states do) you will be collecting taxes any time you sell to the final user of your product, but not when you sell to someone who then sells your product to the final user.

Wholesale selling means that you always sell to someone who, in turn, sells to the public—as with a grocer or a nursery. Your state, county or town may charge you a fee or license to do business, but you don't collect or pay sales taxes for or to them as long as you only sell wholesale. When we get to the part about selling potted herbs, we'll talk a little more about the sales tax at that time, as you may end up selling herbs retail from your back yard.

I operate under a town license costing $42 per year and have a low-cost state business/tax number, called a Resale Number, that allows me to make business purchases at wholesale. It also means that I collect taxes only for any retail sales that I make. I must pay state sales taxes on any books sold by mail order to individual customers in my own state. These are the only licenses, business taxes and fees that I have had to contend with in many years of business. If my business were quite large, other taxes would apply.

Your state, county and/or town fees may be a little different, of course, but they won't amount to much as long as you stay small. Call your own town or county office and ask them about licenses needed for operating a small business.

To find out the business licensing agency of your state, look at the state license posted in any store. The agency name will be there. Give the agency a call. They will explain this to you and send you information in the mail. Don't be intimidated by these steps; they are necessary and relatively simple.

One other person who may be helpful to you in all of this is your county agricultural agent. The same rules will apply to you in selling herbs to your grocer as would apply if you were selling zucchini or rhubarb to your grocer. The county agricultural agents have a wealth of information; give them a call if you can't quite figure out how to start, or which laws would apply to you with what you envision doing. (This assumes that you still have a county agent, a government program fast disappearing as I write this in 1995.)

As far as zoning is concerned, there is also a difference between wholesaling and retailing. If you're dealing with retail customers, zoning really counts. Neighborhoods can get up in arms about a small business setting up in a residential area, if there are customers coming and going all the time. On the other hand, if you're going to be taking your herbs to market, there should be no zoning problems at all. And no zoning problems connected with growing culinary herbs for the local grocers or restaurants. I'll talk a little more about zoning issues in the section on growing and selling potted herbs from your back yard.

BILLING DETAILS

One of the first things to do is order a rubber stamp with your company name, address, and telephone number on it. You'll need this for your invoices. It could also be used on your first labels. If you should choose to also operate a potted herb business, as I describe later in the book, the rubber stamp will be helpful with that.

At your local office supply or drug store, you can buy a book of duplicate invoices. In my area, they come in a little blue colored book of 50 sets for just over two dollars. Use your rubber

Here's an example of a simple invoice for a store account. Use a rubber stamp at the top. Using one line per delivery, you can do 4 to 8 deliveries with one invoice.

stamp across the top of the original copy (which the store will end up keeping) and insert the carbon paper behind that first sheet to make a copy for your records. Each invoice can be used for four to eight deliveries of fresh cut herbs to one store or restaurant.

The important thing to remember is to have someone who works at the business sign for each and every delivery. Have them sign their name or initial along the day's delivery line instead of at the bottom of the invoice. After a few deliveries, I add up the column on the right and turn in the invoice to the produce manager, chef or bookkeeper.

Many stores and restaurants will want to pay you immediately, either with a check or cash out of the cash drawer. For those who want credit, I always show terms on the invoice as "Net 10 days." That means that I expect to be paid the full amount within 10 days.

One word of warning: I would be a little more careful about extending credit to small restaurants (especially if they're rather new) than to stores or markets. Don't be afraid to say, *"I'm the world's smallest company, and need to keep my money coming in while I get started. Please pay me weekly."*

The easiest way to handle any take-backs is to subtract them from your delivery total. If you take in 24 fresh herb packets and pick up three unsold ones that look unappetizing, charge for 21 packets on your invoice entry for that day. This is the simplest, yet adequate, billing method you can use to start out with. You don't need to send additional statements. If your store hasn't paid you in 10 to 20 days, go in and talk with them. Monthly statements are an additional expense you don't need. Keep in close touch with your accounts, not letting them get behind in their payments to you.

TAXES

There are many interesting possibilities about this business where taxes are concerned. The important thing to remember starting out is to keep very good records of any purchases and any expense you incur: seeds, plants, pots, soil, plastic bags, labels, invoices, etc. Your watering cost and delivery costs are deductible, of course. Home-based businesses can have many other tax advantages, but that's another complicated subject beyond the scope of this book. Suffice to say that it's definitely worth looking into with a tax accountant once your business reaches any real size and financial success.

🌿 🌿 🌿 A Potted Herb Business

The other small herb business that is easy to begin in your back yard is that of growing and selling potted herbs. This can fit in very well with the culinary herb business. It can also be done on its own, as a stand alone herb business. Just as with the culinary herb business, there are many forces in society constantly stimulating the public's urge to purchase and plant herbs in their gardens—even in their window sills.

The craft and fragrance herbs are in ever greater demand as more and more people are caught up in the everyday pleasure of herbs. Spend a little time browsing through magazines at a large newsstand, and you will easily spot the continual promotion of craft and fragrance plants: from blending potpourris or herbal vinegar, to crafting wreaths or tussie mussies—this field seems truly limitless.

There is also a growing demand for special landscaping, or ground cover herbs. You could consider building up a backyard business around just those special plants, the thymes, woodruff, and the chamomiles, for instance, that you could sell by the tray-full to home gardeners, landscape businesses and nurseries alike.

Medicinal herbs are also beginning to get more and more attention in the media, and I feel certain there will be an especially strong push towards these medicinal plants in the years to come. The professional herbalists in America are starting to work out their problems with Congress and the FDA and are also starting to be taken more seriously by the American public, who are busy searching for a more holistic approach to their own health care. Every day more people are seeking out herbal preparations at their health food store; and more people will be trying to grow their own herbs, as herbalists go around the country teaching people how to make their own tinctures, salves and simple medications.

For our purposes, all of this promotion and political maneuvering leads inevitably to small business opportunities as the American consumer decides, in one household after another, to get more involved with herbs. They want green, live plants. They love to buy from a local supplier—a local expert, if you will—and that's the opportunity that can be had in every town in the country: local growers meeting that growing need.

The possibilities are there for both wholesale and retail herb businesses—or for a small business that does a little of each.

WHOLESALE AND RETAIL PLANT SELLING

The very first question you must face if you want to consider herb retailing from your back yard, is one of zoning. Do you live in a place where neighbors will be bothered by the increased traffic of people coming to buy your plants? Or will you do all your retail plant selling at farmers' markets, or to nurseries or hardware stores, in which case your zoning is probably of no importance whatsoever.

The recent burgeoning of home-based businesses has been accompanied by a supply of repeated nightmare tales about people who are sued, taken to court, harassed and generally made miserable while trying to earn money where they live. The thousands and thousands of people who successfully (and peacefully) run home-based businesses, even in restricted zones, never make interesting news—until and unless the trouble starts.

Many communities are now acknowledging this change in livelihood patterns around the country and are starting to make a few changes in the zoning laws. Perhaps you can lead your own community in efforts along these lines. But this whole question of zoning is an issue that absolutely must be taken seriously by anyone considering a retail operation in their home. You need to find out your property zoning, the attitudes of your neighbors, and the rules that will apply to anything you decide to do.

Growing plants in your back yard to take away and sell through someone else's store would be considered wholesale selling. Few restrictions would apply to what you do at home in that case. That is also true if you plan to sell your plants at a farmers' market.

Growing plants and selling them from your back yard or home would be considered a retail business. You would need to be very aware of your zoning and the restrictions that may apply for such a business. You would also have to charge taxes (if your state has a retail sales tax) and probably have a license to operate the business.

🌿 🌿 🌿

First let's talk a little about the opportunities for some kind of small wholesale herb plant business. You'll notice how many stores (drug stores, hardware stores, etc.) that carry no plants whatsoever during most of the year, will manage to have a few trays of plant starts during the spring. Those storekeepers know that even their non-gardening customers find those first true signs of spring irresistible. Those same storekeepers might welcome a tray or two of your well marked herbs to sell every spring.

Your local garden center and nursery might also welcome your herbs, even year-round, especially if they are well cared for and haven't suffered the stress of long distance shipping. Chances are your local garden center buys many of their plants from the same supplier used by the garden center just down the freeway, or in the next town. Their herb choices may be very limited, and they often cannot meet any special orders for their local customers. If the big supplier offers only one or two kinds of mint, when there are scores of possibilities, offers only basic culinary herbs, when fragrance and medicinal herbs are being asked for every day, that garden center owner will be very open to your offer to supply potted herbs.

Your marketing efforts in such a potted herb business would be very similar to those I outlined in selling culinary herbs, with one or two important exceptions.

Find out the buyer responsible for the purchasing of herbs.

Take them a sample or two of your efforts.

Offer to try to meet special orders for unusual herbs.

Offer a reasonable wholesale price.

(I deal with pricing further on.)

These would NOT be consignment sales. The store is responsible for taking care of the plants and selling them. You would not take back any that do not sell. Once you have made the sale, keep an eye on the plants to see that they are watered, well marked and well displayed. This may sometimes involve even offering to do a little watering—especially if the store doesn't usually sell plants year-round, and they are very busy in the springtime. (In a real nursery or garden center, the watering is usually handled on a much more regular basis.) But don't make a nuisance of yourself, as your herbs are but a very tiny part of their whole retailing effort. By making a lot of special demands on the storekeepers, you can probably guarantee that your plants won't be welcome there the next year.

For such store sales, bill them as you would for culinary herbs. List your terms as net 10 days. Again, that means that the total amount of the bill is due and payable in 10 days. I wouldn't worry if you don't get paid until they do their regular accounts payable each month, but oftentimes a store will understand the cash flow problems of a very small operator like yourself and will make an effort to pay you faster than their normal accounts—sometimes even on delivery.

It is important to remember that this little wholesale business may take place in only a very few months, even in a few weeks, during springtime. That means being prepared early and having plenty of herbs to offer during those early spring days when the level of interest from gardeners can sometimes seem quite frantic. By June you'll start to wonder where everyone went.

❧ ❧ ❧

To run a small backyard retail operation is also fairly straightforward, assuming you are in the right zone for it. You need a little sign out front, some sales receipts to give to your customers, plus some counter height surfaces on which to place your plants.

Watering is probably the most time consuming (and important) chore you'll have. If you're still fairly new to gardening, this is probably one of the toughest lessons to learn: that these little pots of green are alive and in need of daily watching and some care. They won't holler at you to be watered; they'll simply fold up and die if you neglect them enough.

The other major problem for a backyard seller is that of opening hours. Before you invite the public into your yard to make purchases, you need to think hard about how much time you wish to remain open. Are you intending to be at home every day, all day? Or can you limit it to certain days or hours? What about weekends? Maybe you'd be content with only weekends for just a few weeks in the spring. That means getting the word out with posters, classified ads, or whatever works in your area to get the attention you need.

Small backyard herb sellers often end up adding craft items or their other homemade herb items to sell along with their plants. Sometimes they even end up with a full-fledged Herb Farm. Wouldn't that be fun?

PRICING

In my area, the following retail herb plant prices are in effect as of this writing.

Small (2.5" to 4") pots of herbs retail in our area for about $1.89 to $2.99 per pot, with special herbs, such as bay laurel, going for about $5 in a small pot.

Larger pots (commonly called one gallon size) retail for $3 to $7 per pot. Very slow growing, difficult to start plants, such as the bay laurel, will always draw a higher price. So will unusual varieties, or herbs turned into standards; special hanging pots of herbs,

mixed pots, anything unusual that the customer will not be seeing at every store where plants are sold, will always draw a higher
price. Sometimes new growers can consider specializing in some
of these unusual plantings of herbs, which can be sold both wholesale and retail, rather than trying to compete with basic spring
starts.

The important thing is to look around and see what's out there
in your area and where you can sense a little niche opening for
something you'd like to do. Check your own region carefully, to
see what prices prevail, and realize that you need to be within the
same range, knowing that if you keep your quality very high you
can always charge a little more than the average area price.

Very large wholesale growers in my area now are charging
retailers about 95 cents an herb by the tray full. These are from
growers who also sell a great variety of other plants besides herbs,
and who only carry a fairly limited variety of herbs—usually only
the most popular sellers. No delivery is included.

The large specialty wholesale herb grower in my area (who
only sells herbs) is now charging between 80 cents and $1.50 for
a small pot of herbs, depending both on the size (2.5" or 3.5") and
the type of herb. For gallon pots, the wholesale price runs from
$2 to $4 per pot.

This seems a reasonable price area to be in. I would recommend that you wholesale your herbs for $1.15 to $1.25 per small
plant if you are selling to your local garden center. In my opinion,
the work is just not worth doing for less. You'll learn as you go
along which herbs are very easily grown and which are slow or
difficult to grow.

You can charge different prices based on the type of herbs,
and whatever price you start out at, you can change your prices
as you go along. You can also offer special deals, quantity prices,
or any other prices you feel make your work worthwhile. And
the wonderful thing about any perennial herbs you grow is that if
you don't sell them one year you can hold them over, pot them
up into a larger pot and charge more money the next year. That's
of course not true for the annuals, which must be sold fairly quickly

after you get them ready to sell. One saving grace for annual herbs that don't sell is that they can be harvested and dried, if only for your own use.

WHAT TO GROW

The following list of herbs is a good beginning list to consider if you wish to take up growing potted herbs to sell. It is by no means complete, but just learning to grow these herbs will take considerable time and effort on your part. These are the herbs that can grow in almost any area of the country, and can involve you completely in the subject of herbs and their uses. These are also the plants that are in demand everywhere in the country. I have left out any herbs that could be considered dangerous or even controversial.

I have also left out two herbs known for their high prices and great demand: namely, goldenseal and ginseng. Both are considered difficult plants to cultivate successfully, although there is research being done on both plants towards the goal of making them commercially viable plants to grow. If these plants are especially interesting to you, take a look at the reference section in the back of this book to find how to learn more about them.

A Partial List of
HERBS
& Their Primary Uses

(An asterisk means a very popular herb, easily sold.)

Common Name	Botanical	Culinary/Tea	Craft/Fragrance	Medicinal
Angelica	*Angelica*	•		
Anise	*Pimpinella anisum*	•	•	•
*Basil	*Ocimum basilicum*	•	•	•
*Bay	*Laurus nobilis*	•	•	
Bee balm	*Monarda didyma*	•	•	•
Borage	*Borago officinialis*	•		•
Calendula	*Calendula officinalis*	•	•	•
Caraway	*Carum carvi*	•		•
*Catnip	*Nepeta cataria*		•	•
Cayenne	*Capsicum annum*	•		•
*Chamomile, Ger.	*Matricaria recutita*	•	•	•
*Chamomile, Eng.	*Chamaemelum nobile*	•	•	•
Chervil	*Anthriscus cerefolium*	•		
Chicory	*Cichorium intybus*	•		
*Chives	*Allium schoenoprasum*	•		
*Dill	*Anethum graveolens*	•		
*Echinacea	*E. purpurea, E. angustifolia*			•
Fennel	*Foeniculum vulgare*	•		•
Feverfew	*Tanacetum parthenium*		•	•
*Garlic	*Allium sativum*	•	•	•
Hops	*Humulus lupulus*	•	•	•
Horehound	*Marrubium vulgare*	•		•
Horseradish	*Armoracia rusticana*	•		•

A Partial List of
HERBS 🌿 🌿 🌿
& Their Primary Uses

(An asterisk means a very popular herb, easily sold.)

Common Name	Botanical	Culinary/Tea	Craft/Fragrance	Medicinal
Hyssop	*Hyssopus officinalis*	•	•	•
*Lavenders	*Lavandula*	•	•	•
*Lemon Balm	*Melissa officinalis*	•	•	•
Lemon verbena	*Aloysia triphylla*	•	•	
Lovage	*Levisticum officinale*	•		•
*Marjoram	*Origanum majorana*	•	•	
*Mints	*Mentha*	•	•	•
*Oregano	*Origanum*	•	•	•
*Parsley	*Petroselinum*	•		
Passionflower	*Passiflora incarnata*	•	•	•
*Pennyroyal	*Mentha pulegium*	•	•	
*Rosemary	*Rosmarinus*	•	•	•
*Sage	*Salvia officinalis*	•	•	•
Salad burnet	*Poterium sanguisorba*	•		
Savories	*Satureja hortensis, S. montana*	•		
*Scented geraniums	*Pelargonium*	•	•	
Sweet Cicely	*Myrrhis odorata*	•	•	
Sweet woodruff	*Galium odoratum*	•	•	
*French tarragon	*Artemisia drancunculus*	•		
*Thymes	*Thymus*	•	•	•
Valerian	*Valeriana officinalis*		•	•
Wormwoods	*Artemisia*		•	•
Yarrow	*Achillea millefolium*		•	•

SUPPLIES NEEDED FOR A POTTED HERB BUSINESS

The primary supplies to be considered in a potted herb business are soil, pots and markers. And the first thing you'll no doubt want to ask is:

Where can I buy some of these supplies cheaper than at the regular retail price? I don't want very large wholesale quantities—in case I decide to remain as a very small backyard grower, or in case I decide that this little horticulture business is not for me.

In the reference section at the back of this book I will list some specific companies that will supply you by mail for some of this, probably at less than retail prices. But there are no doubt companies in your own region that will do the same, once you contact them.

The first thing to do is look in the yellow pages for the largest urban or suburban area closest to you. Look under the listings for Nursery Supplies, wholesale; or Landscaping Supplies, wholesale. Give them a call, explain that you are just starting a small potted herb business and that you want to check prices for potting soil, pots and markers. Ask if they have a catalog to send you. You will need to give them your business name, possibly a tax number, and, in some states, even a plant grower's number that is sometimes required by your state agricultural department. Whatever the state regulations are in your state, this company should let you know during that first phone call just what you'll need in order to purchase wholesale from them. It's an easy way to find out which special rules may exist in your state.

Ask the company what their minimum purchase requirement is, when and if you can visit their warehouse and look at their goods, what their credit requirements are, or if you must deal in cash to begin with (which is most likely). Call every company listed, see which ones are the most friendly and welcoming, as they will be the companies used to dealing with a small time operator like yourself and that will be the most helpful to you.

Remember that there are many small horticultural businesses starting out every day in this country, and some of them will grow to be quite large. The wholesale companies you contact also know that and, if they are run well, will welcome you as a potential large customer right from the beginning. Don't be shy about calling, and don't be blown away by the occasional rude clerk who may be manning the phones on the day you call. Friendly persistence will get you the answers and the help you need.

Potting Soil

Most new commercial herb growers begin with bags of potting soil from their local garden center, farm supply or hardware store, when they first start potting up herbs for sale. Another place to look for an even better price would be at the very large discount stores springing up all around the country. The problem is, often these stores only carry such items during the spring season, when they're very salable.

Perhaps you are thinking that you can start with soil from your own garden, but this is usually much less desirable than commercial potting soil. Easily carried soil fungi can quickly cause your tiny seedlings to die. Commercial potting soils are sterilized.

Yes, there are ways to sterilize your soil at home—even in your oven (which will smell up your kitchen in a hurry). You can also sterilize soil in a greenhouse or garden with extra plumbing and supplies. But, to get yourself off to a fast start, I recommend that you use commercial potting soil to begin with. The nursery supply houses will carry bags of this soil, usually at lower prices than your local farm supply or hardware store.

When your business increases enough, it may pay you to learn to mix your own soil. But I have noticed that even the largest companies I've visited have potting soil delivered in large trucks as the most cost effective way to get this major supply.

Pots

There are many types and sizes of pots available these days, and little information about which ones customers prefer. Clay pots are too expensive to consider using when you are starting out, so the basic choice is between the plastic pots and the molded pulp/ peat pots that can be planted in the ground with the plant.

In transplanting into the garden, I've come to suspect that the pulp pots hold back the plant's growth a little, and that the pot itself seems to absorb water while often leaving the soil inside the pot a little dry. These are only guesses. I would recommend that you choose whichever type of pot you are more comfortable working with.

There's a lot to be said for adding the pot to the soil instead of it eventually going to the landfill, and I do hate the build-up of plastic pots that can occur in growers' back yards. Both types of pots degrade when left to the weather. If you re-use pots, be sure to wash them thoroughly so as not to spread soil borne plant diseases.

If you start with basic plastic pots, the next decision is about pot sizes for selling herbs. The usual approach is to grow a small starter plant in a 2.5", 3.5" or 4" pot, and then a larger size, commonly called a gallon pot, that is usually a 5" or 6" diameter size.

The wholesale prices in my area right now for inexpensive plastic pots of these sizes are:

2.5" size	Approx. $20 for a case of 1,000 pots
3.5"	Approx. $25 for a case of 500 pots
4"	Approx. $42 for a case of 500 pots

Pots of better quality of plastic go up from these, but only by a penny or two a pot. Your small pots should cost you less than six or seven cents apiece, and often you can get them for two or three cents apiece.

The so-called gallon size will cost you between 15 and 25 cents each, depending on the quality.

Pulp pots cost a little more.

Markers

Look in the reference section for places to buy plant markers in small quantities by mail, but they are also available at your regional nursery or florist supplier.

At our local wholesalers, they cost around one cent each, in lots of 1,000.

When you use white markers that you make up yourself, be sure to use a sharp pointed, waterproof laundry pen (available in any office supply). The helpful information to put on a marker is the common name; whether it's a perennial, annual or biennial; whether it likes sun, shade or both; and how tall it might grow. That may be too much to put on a marker, but do the best you can. You need only use the common name unless you think there may be some confusion in the customer's mind—with the savories, for instance, or with tarragon to reassure the customer that it is the French tarragon you're selling, not the much less desirable Russian variety.

Plastic Plant Trays

For even a small wholesale or retail herb business, you'll need some standard plastic trays for carrying and displaying herbs. You can retrieve or exchange these trays at any store you sell to. As of this writing, such trays are priced at about 50 cents each in my area.

✿ ✿ ✿ *More About Growing Herbs*

There are so many wonderful and detailed herb gardening books out these days that I'll limit this section to the ideas about growing herbs that I've found to be extra important, and then give a few recommendations for gardening books in the reference section.

If you are not yet a gardener, you must face that honestly and start from that point. It means you'll probably have to spend a lot of time and effort in learning some gardening basics before you can hope to earn an income at this. It's not so difficult, but it is definitely not something you can ignore in your consideration of an herb business.

It always gives me a kick to think I may be starting some people along the garden path for the first time in their lives, as gardening is one of life's most special experiences. It can tie you into your place on this planet in a way almost no other activity can. To think that you can also learn to earn some of your livelihood from it sometimes seems almost too good to be true. I have been unable to garden during some years, and those years were never my best ones. Learn about the Master Gardener Program in your area if you are a beginner.

SEED STARTING INFORMATION

If you grow herbs to sell as fresh cut culinary herbs, you will be planting the annuals, like basil and sweet marjoram, every year, and tending your perennials, like chives and tarragon, as they come up again in the spring. Seed starting information will be the same for these herbs as for those you sell in pots.

The key points I'd like to make to novice seed planters are:

1. **Add bottom heat to seeds** and
2. **Keep them moist**.

I grow seeds in three ways:

1. I purchase small, compressed peat pellets (size 9) and put them in small trays or plastic egg cartons. After wetting the pellets overnight (they increase in height) I put two or three seeds in each pellet. I then put a little piece of hardware cloth over a small heating cable (available in garden centers and hardware stores) and put the trays or egg cartons on top of the hardware cloth. That protects the cartons from burning or melting.

I cover each tray or egg carton with plastic wrap after they are planted. That will keep the seeds moistened until germination. I check the seeds every day or so to see if they are germinating, and as soon as most of the seeds do, I remove the plastic wrap and move the plants into good light. They can remain in the peat pellets for at least a few weeks if I keep them well watered. They can then be potted up or put

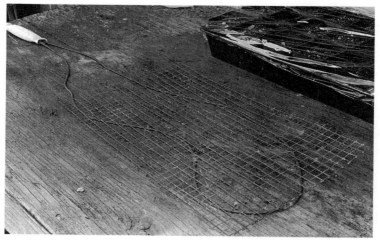

Heating cable and hardware cloth

into the garden if the time is right for planting out. This method is handy when you only want to end up with a few plants of one kind.

2. The same method can be used for small pots, using damp potting soil to within 1/2" of the top. Add the seeds, cover with plastic wrap, and place in a plastic tray over a heating cable, as above. Leave the heating cable on until germination.

3. When I want to grow a lot of one plant (as with basil) I use a shallow plastic or wooden tray filled with damp potting soil. I first make certain there are drainage holes in the tray. I sprinkle on the seeds, then add a thin covering of soil, cover with plastic wrap, and place the tray over the hardware cloth and heating cable. After the seeds have germinated, I remove the wrap (which has kept the moisture in) put the tray in good light and let the plants grow until they have at least four real leaves. Then I transplant into small pots where they can remain until the weather is good for planting out.

Propagation of Herbs

Many herbs are easily propagated, so once you have an established collection of herb plants, these become your "mother plants" from which you can propagate many, many new plants to sell every year. This is usually done by fairly simple techniques of cutting stems from the mother plants at the proper time, putting them in a clean medium (such as sand), keeping them shaded and moist, and waiting for new roots to establish. In the reference section, I recommend some books that deal quite specifically with this subject .

Plant division is another technique you'll learn to increase your plant supply. With plants like chives, for instance, you can easily turn a few plants into a multitude for only the cost of soil and pots.

If you choose to do both a culinary cut herb business and a potted herb business from the same garden, it will take a little more room than if you only do one business or the other.

A Place to Start Your Seeds

Do you have to have a greenhouse to make a successful small business of herbs? Not at all, but you do have to figure out a weather-protected place in which to start your seeds early. It's also very nice to have a place to winter over some tender plants: scented geraniums, for instance. Once my own first efforts outgrew the sunny spots indoors, I built a little seed starting place outside with bales of hay on three sides, covered over and fronted with old sliding glass doors. I have often helped friends put up plastic walls around porches or carports in order to be able to start their seeds early.

I now have a lovely greenhouse and would wish one for every serious gardener. In the meantime, use your imagination to create a space, and **remember the importance of fresh air** to any enclosed space where you put plants. A modern greenhouse has automatic fans and vents to keep the space from overheating. But only you can remember every day to get fresh air into any space you build for plants, and then to cover it again for frosty nights.

Fertilizers and Pesticides

Herbs are rather easily grown plants with few problems. I use compost in my garden and sometimes spread chicken manure laden sawdust from chicken barns through my gardens. I never see the need to use commercial fertilizers on the herbs in the garden. If you are growing potted herbs, you'll want to consider using an organic liquid fertilizer such as seaweed or fish emulsion.

Herbs that have been sprayed with insecticides seem not worth selling to me. I sell unwashed herbs so that they'll stay fresher longer in the packets. I wouldn't want to sell herbs covered with poisons. I do have to use slug bait near the sorrel bed, but otherwise it's better to sell organically grown herbs and to advertise them as such on your label.

Organically grown food is certainly what health conscious people are demanding more and more of these days, so why not start out your herb business that way to begin with.

🌿 🌿 🌿 *Other Herb Business Possibilities*

There are also other businesses that these efforts can lead to, depending on your time, space, interest and resources. Herb growing can also lead you into herbal products, such as herb vinegar, dried herb seasoning packets, sachets, herb pillows, etc. I've found fresh culinary herbs and potted herbs to be the most profitable for me, but it's also possible to include additional sidelines as you learn more about these remarkable plants.

In 1994, I wrote another book called *Herbs For Sale*, that tells in great detail about many of these other herbal businesses. I traveled the country visiting many different kinds of herb ventures. The book details a very large cut herb business, a large potted herb business, one in mixed salad greens, and several other herb businesses that these beginning efforts may encourage you to consider. You can get that book through your library or order it from the back of this book

One thing will happen after it becomes known that you have an herb business: you'll soon be considered an "expert" on herbs and will be asked to speak at garden clubs, horticultural societies, garden centers, cooking classes, etc. That can be fun and it also offers a chance to tell where your fresh herbs are being sold. Taking up the study of herbs along with the study of gardening can easily keep a person occupied for life.

I encourage you to give some time to the reference section that follows. If you live in an isolated area, as I do, this section can show you how to get in touch with herbalists and herbal information all over the country.

✤ ✤ ✤

I would be pleased to hear from any of you. I wish you good luck in your endeavors, and hope this information continues to be of help to you.

✹ ✹ ✹ *References and Resources*

If this little book has helped to inspire you to take up an herb business, this reference section should provide some additional specific help in answering further questions you may have. Take a few minutes to look through the whole section.

I've tried to list books that are available through your library; most magazines will send you a sample copy for the asking; most associations and companies have free brochures you can ask for to gain a little more information about their products. In other words, there's no need to spend money now on any of these listings. But, as you get involved in herbs and want to learn more, here are the resources you can look to for further help.

HERB ASSOCIATIONS

International Herb Association. Formerly known as the International Herb Growers and Marketing Association (IHGMA), this is the primary commercial herb association in the country. A friendly, active organization, they sponsor a large conference every year, plus regional seminars during the year. You might not want to consider joining this immediately, but send for a sample of their newsletter to see what they are about. 1202 Allanson Rd., Mundelein, IL 60060. 708-949-4372.

Herb Society of America. First formed in 1933, this is a non-commercial membership group that sponsors gardens, tours, herb research and education. Membership is by recommendation or sponsorship. 9019 Kirtland-Chardon Rd., Mentor, OH 44060. 216-256-0514.

HERB PUBLICATIONS AND DIRECTORIES

The Business of Herbs

An important small business journal for herbalists. Published bi-monthly, it covers many types of herb businesses. Ask for a sample copy. They also publish the *Herb Resource Directory* which lists herb businesses around the country. RR2, Box 246, Shevlin, MN 56676. 218-657-2478.

HerbalGram

Published quarterly by the American Botanical Council and the Herb Research Foundation, this is the primary national journal about the chemical properties of herbs. Includes worldwide studies of herbs and herbal medicines. Highly informative. See a sample copy at your library, or contact PO Box 201660, Austin, TX 78720. 512-331-8868.

The Herbal Connection

Another good bi-monthly newsletter about herbs and business, with emphasis on marketing and financial aspects. Also publishes *The Green Pages* listing herb businesses. 3343 Nolt Rd., Lancaster, PA 17601.

American Ginseng Trends

A newsletter for the ginseng industry: growing, harvesting, marketing, etc. PO Box 1982, Wausau, WI 54402.

Potpourri from Herbal Acres

An eclectic newsletter with the accent on using herbs in the kitchen and crafts. Written by the author of *The Pleasure of Herbs*. PO Box 428LS, Washington Crossing, PA 18977.

Wild Foods Forum

All about food foraging, and fun to read. 4 Carlisle Way NE, Atlanta, GA 30308.

GREENHOUSE SUPPLIES

Start with a free catalog from a greenhouse materials supply company. Try **Charley's Greenhouse Supply**, 1569 Memorial Highway, Mt. Vernon, WA 98273, or **Gardener's Supply Co.,** 128 Intervale Rd., Burlington, VT 05401. Both companies read and review the latest and best books on greenhouse building and growing techniques.

POTTED HERB SUPPLIES

Send for a catalog from: **A. M. Leonard, Inc.,** PO Box 816, Piqua, OH 45356, **Park Seed Wholesale**, Cokesbury Road, Greenwood, SC 29647, or **Mellinger's Inc.,** 2310 W. South Rage Road, North Lima, OH 44452.

MASTER GARDENER PROGRAM

See your Agricultural Extension Agent, or check with your library for a copy of the Directory of Master Gardener Programs published by Master Gardeners International, 2904 Cameron Mills Rd., Alexandria, VA 22302.

MAIL ORDER HERB PLANT AND SEED SOURCES

Fedco Seeds Co-op
52 Mayflower Hill Dr., Waterville, ME 04901 (S)

Johnny's Selected Seeds
Foss Hill Rd., Albion, ME 04910 (S)

Nichols Garden Nursery
1190 No. Pacific Hwy., Albany, OR 97321 (S&P and they also sell elephant garlic for planting.)

Park Seeds
Greenwood, SC 29647 (S&P)

Pinetree Garden Seeds
Rte. 100, New Gloucester, ME 04260 (S)

Richters
Box 26, Goodwood, Ont., Canada L0C 1A0 (S)

Taylor's Herb Gardens, Inc.
1535 Lone Oak Rd., Vista, CA 92084 (P)

See *Gardening By Mail*
by Barbara J. Barton, available at your library.

RECOMMENDED BOOKS

Go first to your library and see what they offer. Almost every publishing company in America has put out at least one volume on herbs. There are even more selections on general and organic gardening. If you are just beginning, almost anything you read will be helpful. What follows are currently my own personal favorites. These books should also be available through your library system. They may not be on the shelf, but they can probably be obtained through your regional library system. Ask your local librarian for help in finding them.

Herbal Renaissance
by Steven Foster. Gibbs Smith, Salt Lake City, 1993. (Includes up-to-date information on goldenseal and ginseng.)

Growing Great Garlic
by Ron Engeland. Filaree Productions, Okanogan, WA, 1991. (He also sells organically grown garlic for small commercial production. Filaree Farm, Rt. 1, Box 162, Okanogan, WA 98840.)

Growing & Using Herbs Successfully
by Betty E. M. Jacobs. Select Books, Mountain View, MO, 1976. (Good information on propagating herbs.)

The Complete Medicinal Herbal
by Penelope Ody. Dorling Kindersley, New York, 1993. (A splendid introduction to simple herbal medicine making at home.)

Park's Success With Herbs
Park Seeds, Greenwood, SC.

Culinary Herbs
James A. Duke. Trado Medic Books, NY, 1985.

Growing Herbs from Seed, Cutting and Root
Interweave Press, Loveland, CO, 1995. (I haven't read this yet myself, but the reviews have been glowing, and this is just the information you need to start a potted herb business.)

RECOMMENDED BUSINESS BOOKS
Growing a Business
Paul Hawken. Simon & Schuster, NY, 1987.

Homemade Money
Barbara Brabec. Betterway Publications, VA, 1984.

Small Time Operator
Bernard Kamoroff, CPA. Bell Springs Publishing, CA, 1984.

Index

Profits from Your Backyard Herb Garden

FLOWERS FOR SALE
Growing & Marketing Cut Flowers, Backyard to Small Acreage

by Lee Sturdivant

The first guide on how you can start a cut flower business from your back yard, this book leads you easily into the business world of growing and selling flowers. First come **complete details** on how you can start and operate a simple bouquet business, even from a small garden, no matter where you live. You then visit flower growers and buyers, a U-Pick flower farm, Saturday Markets, flower auctions, plus wholesale florists and growers in several states. You'll learn from their experience and their advice will help you get started. In the last part of the book, *The Cut Flower Catalog* lists hundreds of varieties of perennials, annuals, bulbs, tubers, trees, vines, shrubs and herbs that can be used successfully as commercial cut flowers.

> 200 pages. $14.95 + s & h
> ISBN # 9621638-1-1

The Reviewers comment on FLOWERS FOR SALE:

"*Flowers For Sale* is an easy and entertaining read, packed with hard information and instructive anecdotes for the beginning flower grower."

> *Growing Edge Magazine*

"...provides a great starting point for new commercial flower growers and includes some unique marketing ideas that even established growers can find useful."

> Judy Laushman, Executive Director
> Assoc. of Specialty Cut Flowers, Inc.

"Helps get you started selling what you're already growing, then expands with you as your confidence grows. Highly recommended."

> Johnny's Selected Seeds Catalog

"If you have a knack for growing flowers and are wondering about turning part of the back yard into a cash crop...you should read *Flowers For Sale*. It offers sound advice."
Dick Tracy, *Sacramento Bee*

Flowers For Sale has been selected by Better Homes & Gardens Book Club and by Mother Earth News Bookshelf.

See Order Coupon at end of book.

HERBS FOR SALE
Growing and Marketing Herbs,
Herbal Products & Herbal Know-How

by Lee Sturdivant

Interested in an herbal business? Here's the first guide to the burgeoning small business world of herbs; it offers you an overview of where you might fit into this growing American passion for herbs. Detailed, advice-filled visits with small backyard herb growers and large greenhouse herb growers; Herb Farm owners, both beginners and long time experts; wildcrafters, garlic growers, herb product makers, teachers and writers about herbs from all across the country. Each chapter is followed by a complete reference section about where to get supplies and ever more herbal information. A thorough resource for the herb professional, both the beginner and the more advanced. 250 pages $14.95 + s. & h. ISBN # 9621635-2-X

The Reviewers comment on *HERBS FOR SALE:*
"Lee takes you on the coast-to-coast market research tour you know you should do before starting a business. This is a truly useful book."
Growing For Market

"At last we have the definitive book for herb-lovers looking to go from a hobby to a career. ...illustrate(s) how to stay profitable and solve problems, as well as how to market and grow herbs...The reference guides following each division are especially helpful."
Herbal Gazette

If you are in the "wanna be" stage of owning an herb business, and need help to zero in on the right path to take, you will find this book **invaluable!** ...The reference sections at the end of each chapter are so thorough that they alone are worth the price of the book!
Phyllis Shaudys,
Pot Pourri From Herbal Acres.

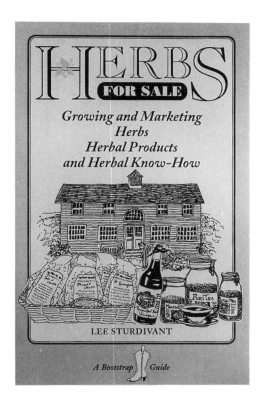

Growing and Marketing
Herbs
Herbal Products
and Herbal Know-How

LEE STURDIVANT

A Bootstrap Guide

"Sturdivant has mastered the three *"I"*s: she *I*nvolves, *I*nspires & *I*nstructs. Along the way, she has a keen sense of marketing. "
Fedco Seed Catalog

"…essential reading for anyone interested in owning and operating an herb business…an extremely valuable reference for newcomers and experienced business people alike. I highly recommend this book!"
Paula Oliver, Ed. *Bu$iness of Herbs*

Herbs For Sale has been selected by
Organic Gardening Book Club
and by Mother Earth News Bookshelf

See Order Coupon at end of book.

BOOTSTRAP GUIDES ORDER FORM

QTY	TITLE	PRICE	TOTAL
	FLOWERS FOR SALE: *Growing and Marketing Cut Flowers,* *Backyard to Small Acreage* 225 pages	$14.95	
	HERBS FOR SALE: *Growing and Marketing Herbs,* *Herbal Products and Herbal* *Know-How* 250 pages	$14.95	
	PROFITS FROM YOUR *BACKYARD HERB GARDEN* *A First Steps Guide* 120 pages	$10.95	
	Subtotal		
	Postage and Handling (Add $1.50 for one book, 50¢ for each additional book.)		
	Sales tax (WA residents only, add 7%)		
	Total Enclosed		

I understand that I may return any books for a full refund if not satisfied.

YOUR NAME _____

ADDRESS _____

CITY _____

STATE ZIP _____

DAYTIME PHONE _____

Enclosed is my check payable to San Juan Naturals, or
Please charge my _____ MasterCard _____ Visa

Account No. _____

Exp. Date _____ Signature _____

Mail or Fax to: SAN JUAN NATURALS,
PO Box 642P
Friday Harbor, WA 98250
Toll Free Order Phone: 1-800-770-9070
Fax 206-378-2584

*IF THIS IS A LIBRARY
BOOK, PLEASE
PHOTOCOPY THIS PAGE.
THANK YOU FOR YOUR
ORDER!*

BOOTSTRAP GUIDES ORDER FORM

QTY	TITLE	PRICE	TOTAL
	FLOWERS FOR SALE: *Growing and Marketing Cut Flowers,* *Backyard to Small Acreage* 225 pages	$14.95	
	HERBS FOR SALE: *Growing and Marketing Herbs,* *Herbal Products and Herbal* *Know-How* 250 pages	$14.95	
	PROFITS FROM YOUR *BACKYARD HERB GARDEN* *A First Steps Guide* 120 pages	$10.95	
Subtotal			
Postage and Handling (Add $1.50 for one book, 50¢ for each additional book.)			
Sales tax (WA residents only, add 7%)			
Total Enclosed			

I understand that I may return any books for a full refund if not satisfied.

YOUR NAME _____

ADDRESS _____

CITY _____

STATE ZIP _____

DAYTIME PHONE _____

Enclosed is my check payable to San Juan Naturals, or
Please charge my _____ MasterCard _____ Visa

Account No. _____

Exp. Date _____ Signature _____

Mail or Fax to: SAN JUAN NATURALS,
PO Box 642P
Friday Harbor, WA 98250
Toll Free Order Phone: 1-800-770-9070
Fax 206-378-2584

IF THIS IS A LIBRARY
BOOK, PLEASE
PHOTOCOPY THIS PAGE.
THANK YOU FOR YOUR
ORDER!